"Kelly was in the room when I pitched my first TV series, saw the value of the show, its impact on culture, and therefore was a key advocate for the greenlight that changed my life. Consider this book a gift, and soak up the insight and information she generously offers in these pages."

—MARA BROCK-AKIL, Creator of *Being Mary Jane* and *Girlfriends*

"Everyone trying to break into writing for television is looking for the same thing: practical information and actionable advice. At last, the wait is over. Kelly Edwards has delivered an essential everything-you-need-to-know guide to the business of TV."

—CRAIG MAZIN, Creator and Writer of *Chernobyl*

"Knowing how to pitch well, take notes, and understand the business is the key to success in Hollywood. This book has all of that and more."

—MALCOLM SPELLMAN, Executive Producer of Marvel's *The Falcon and the Winter Soldier*

"As a seasoned industry veteran, even I gained new insight from Kelly's demystifying peek behind the curtain. *The Executive Chair* is a breezy, invaluable and revelatory read for anyone even considering a writing career in Hollywood."

—YVETTE LEE BOWSER, Creator and Executive Producer of *Living Single*

"Kelly Edwards has written the single most concise, practical, and useful book for understanding the TV development process I have ever read. She tells it exactly as it is. No BS, no Hollywood phoniness. I found myself saying, 'Yes, yes!' on every page. If only I had this book years ago. . . ."

—GLEN MAZZARA, Writer/Executive Producer *The Shield*; Showrunner, *The Walking Dead*; Creator/Showrunner, *Damien*

"*The Executive Chair* is an exceptional and comprehensive look at the script development process and the skills it takes to sell a successful series. Kelly Edwards, who has an extraordinary career and sees this process through various lenses, gives a profound glimpse into the process. Information is power, and this book is full of it. If you want to know what it takes to sell a successful series, read, absorb, and put into practice this advice from someone who knows."

—JEN GRISANTI, Story/Career Consultant at JGCI, Speaker, Author, and Writing Instructor

"If you've ever wondered what really goes on behind network/studio doors and how decisions are made on their projects, *The Executive Chair* is a must-read! With laser-like precision, former Hollywood exec Kelly Edwards breaks down everything from behind-the-scenes groundwork to an exec's POV on how internships and volunteering for industry events can lead to follow-up meetings and other door-opening opportunities! Kelly shares her insider knowledge and advice on the value of the perfect pitch, writing the pilot script, how to take notes and successfully navigate the studio/network labyrinth — all with a wink and a reassuring smile!"

—KATHIE FONG YONEDA, Author of *The Script-Selling Game*, Former Studio Exec

"From Getting In to Your Game Plan, Kelly Edwards is right: they don't teach TV development. She does. Essential reading for creating, navigating, and getting your unique material made from the executives' point of view. Very valuable to anyone in the industry."

— DAVE WATSON, Author of *Walkabout Undone*, Editor for *Movies Matter*

"For people interested in Hollywood, how it works and how best to not only break in but make it big, Kelly's book is in a class all its own. Kelly's experiences as a buyer of content, a producer, and as a writer — all told with real humor and through the unique perspective of an African-American woman coming up at a time and in a business that was anything but diverse — make her book *The Executive Chair* an invaluable read and one that's as entertaining as it is informative. It's not just for people trying to make it in entertainment, it's for anyone fascinated with how the sausage gets made in Hollywood and how surprisingly easy it is to learn to get to the top of the Hollywood factory food chain."

— TOM NUNAN, Former Network and Studio President, Oscar-winning
    Executive Producer and Founder of *The Industry Way*

Reading *The Executive Chair* is like having your favorite aunt, who happens to be the head of a TV network, sit at the kitchen table and tell you exactly how things really work. An aunt who wants the best for you and is going to give you all the inside information and strategies you need to succeed as a writer. There's no other book out there like this. Clear and engaging, just the practical specifics on how to network effectively and getting inside the mind of an executive giving notes is going to save you years of confusion and struggle.

— CAROLE KIRSCHNER, Director of the WGA Showrunner Training Program
    and the CBS Diversity Writers Program, and Author of *Hollywood Game Plan:
    How to Land a Job in Film, TV or Digital Entertainment*

If you've ever pitched to an executive at a studio, network, or streamer, and wondered, "What are they really thinking?" Kelly Edwards gives you the answers to that and more in *The Executive's Chair*. She's the real deal, with years of experience at major networks and studios. Her astute advice and tips for getting your foot in the door as an executive to pitching and writing TV Bibles and Series is a treasure-trove of information for up-and-coming writers, producers, and seasoned vets alike. Plus, she's just plain funny, and a straight talker! This should be on every serious-minded content creator's bookshelf.

— RONA EDWARDS, Producer, Author of *I Liked It, Didn't Love It (Screenplay
    Development from the Inside Out* and *The Complete Filmmakers Guide to Film
    Festivals*. Former VP of Creative Affairs for Michael Phillips Productions and
    John Larroquette's Port Street Films.

THE EXECUTIVE CHAIR

A Writer's Guide *to* TV Series Development

KELLY EDWARDS

MICHAEL WIESE PRODUCTIONS

Published by Michael Wiese Productions
12400 Ventura Blvd. #1111
Studio City, CA 91604
(818) 379-8799, (818) 986-3408 (FAX)
mw@mwp.com
www.mwp.com

Cover design by Johnny Ink. www.johnnyink.com
Copyediting by Sarah Beach
Cover photo credit: Daniel Reichert

Manufactured in the United States of America

Copyright © 2021 by Kelly Edwards
First Printing 2021

Library of Congress Cataloging-in-Publication Data

Names: Edwards, Kelly - author.
Title: Executive chair : a writer's guide to TV series development / by
   Kelly Edwards.
Description: Studio City, CA : Michael Wiese Productions, [2021] | Summary:
   "To make compelling television, our industry depends on enthusiastic new
   voices with fresh ideas. While there are plenty of books about the
   mechanics of writing, this is the first time an insider has detailed the
   invaluable TV executive perspective. As key pieces of the entertainment
   puzzle, executives hold institutional wisdom that seldom gets
   disseminated outside network walls. The Executive Chair breaks down the
   business from the gatekeeper's point of view, illuminating the creative
   process used by those who ultimately make the decisions. Whether
   developing a project for the entertainment marketplace or merely probing
   the executive mindset, The Executive Chair dispels myths about the
   creative process and takes the reader through the development of a pilot
   script"– Provided by publisher.
Identifiers: LCCN 2020057248 | ISBN 9781615933303 (trade paperback)
Subjects: LCSH: Television series–Production and direction–United States.
   | Television producers and directors–United States. |
   Executives–United States.
Classification: LCC PN1992.75 .E39 2021 | DDC 791.4502/32–dc23
LC record available at https://lccn.loc.gov/2020057248

CONTENTS

CHAPTER 7

THE PILOT SCRIPT

CHAPTER 8

NOTES

CHAPTER 9

CONGRATS! YOU'VE SOLD YOUR SCRIPT!

CHAPTER 10

FINAL THOUGHTS

DEDICATION

To my family,

whose encouragement, inspiration, and support are
absolutely everything.

FOREWORD

*T*his invaluable book, a gold-mine of industry-wisdom, would have been a godsend to me thirty-five years ago, when I first began knocking on the closed doors of Hollywood.

After graduating from college, it took film school and ten more years of bruised knuckles before I finally got my first real break, directing *Austin Powers, International Man of Mystery*. Before that, I slogged through dozens of freelance gigs — teaching cinematography, shooting art films for friends, editing promo pieces for the Rose Parade. I also worked as a P.A., a sound man, and finally as a writers' assistant, like, forever. I also wrote my own above-average spec scripts, took fruitless meetings, and droned through dozens of so-so pitches. I did finally get hired to write a few scripts, but they were not amazing; I did not paint the town red.

Determined and resilient, I convinced myself that I had plenty of talent and a committed work ethic, so the problem couldn't be me. I blamed the "system" and the "gate keepers;" they just didn't appreciate what I could do for them. If only I'd had Kelly's book to set me straight. A lot of my early mistakes had to do with a lack of appreciation for the collaborative process. And an inability to "read the room." Most development execs, producers, and even assistants you encounter along the way are solid story-crafters, and could directly or indirectly become your collaborators and co-creators, if you would just engage with them enthusiastically, as teammates, rather than defensively, as critics and saboteurs.

Even after I started directing, and I was "in the door," I could have used her chapter on pitching! I once pitched an adaptation of a cult-favorite book to a famous executive producer on the Universal lot. I decided I should tell her ALL the things I loved about the book, and ALL the many nuances in the novel's whole, complex story. For over an hour (nooooo!). I pitched my heart out, flooding the room with way more than enough details about how I would bring the book's richness and humor to the screen. I finally stopped only when I was interrupted by snoring. Yeah. I looked up to see that I had put the exec to sleep. I had knocked her out. Literally. The junior exec in the room — a friend who got me in — glared at me, and then coughed politely to wake her up. Suffice it to say, she did not say "go on," and I did not sell that pitch.

Kelly could have seen that coming. From her wealth of experience, she serves up ideas and useful advice on pitching, collaborating, giving and taking notes, and just generally outsmarting the development system. She has spent her entire career supporting emerging talent and giving them the tools to break in. She doesn't believe in barriers and she wants to kick the doors open whenever and wherever possible. This book is a great starting point for anyone looking to forge a career in this business. Listen to her, and let her mentor you through the pages of this book. You'll walk away with a can-do, collaborative approach to your work and career that will enable you to do your best work with the best people.

Jay Roach
Director/Producer/Writer
Bombshell, Game Change, Meet the Parents

PREFACE

*A*s key decision-makers, executives play an essential role in the television creative process. We buy the scripts, give the notes, approve the casting selections, and hire the crews. We are also the keepers of an enormous amount of Hollywood's institutional wisdom. And while there are plenty of books on the market about writing and producing in the entertainment industry, I've always wondered why there isn't much about the making of television from the executive point of view.

Getting a project from concept to purchase can seem like an insurmountable task. It can take months, if not years, to see a script go from pitch to production. Development execs are trained to look out for signposts, ask certain questions, and steer the project in the right direction. So, what if, instead of keeping our process to ourselves, we actually made getting in easier? What if we gave out the cheat sheet on how to make it as a TV writer in Hollywood?

I've never been a fan of the phrase "I'd like to pick your brain." For me, it always conjured up images of a surgeon poking around in an open skull with a painfully sharp instrument. Nothing I'd ever like to witness, let alone experience. However, it does seem to work in this context. Whenever I speak at conferences, festivals, and events the questions are often the same. How do I get into the industry? Can you give me tips on getting through a pitch? How do I follow up with an executive without being annoying? I got this weird note from someone, what does it mean?

When I first entered the business, I wasn't even aware that there was such a thing as development. I didn't know that before a TV show wound up on air, it started with a pitch, went through rewrites, production, and post-production. As far as I was concerned, the actors made it all up as they went along. But after thirty plus years as an executive, producer, program instructor, and writer, I've seen how things work from a variety of vantage points and think it's high time we opened up the playbook.

If you ask a hundred executives, you may get slightly different answers about their process. This book reflects my personal experience in the industry. Hopefully, it will provide valuable insights to help you blaze a long and prosperous path in this business as you bring your bold ideas to fruition.

My book is open. My brain is yours. Feel free to pick away.

INTRODUCTION

As far as I'm concerned, if you're reasonably intelligent, show up on time, finish what you start, and get along with others, you can have a career in the entertainment business. The writers who make it are the ones who finish their scripts on time. The successful directors are those who follow their films through post. The actors who stick with their craft are the ones who eventually book the jobs. Of course, you have to do the work of perfecting your craft. You must study, practice, and learn the ropes of the industry you want to be a part of, but, as we often say, none of this is brain surgery.

I began my career in entertainment assisting a prominent talent manager, moved over into casting, and then made my way to development and production as a writer's assistant. My first executive job came when I was promoted to Story Editor by Laura Ziskin who, at the time, had a deal with Sony Pictures. Laura had produced *Pretty Woman*[1] and would later go on to kickstart the *Spider-Man*[2] franchise. While at Ziskin Productions, we started shooting *What About Bob?*[3] starring Bill Murray and Richard Dreyfuss. From there, I moseyed over to Garry Marshall's company when he was shooting *Frankie and Johnny*[4] with Al Pacino and Michelle Pfeiffer. If you look closely you can even see me sitting behind Michelle in the first scene

---

[1] https://www.imdb.com/title/tt0100405/
[2] https://www.imdb.com/title/tt0145487/
[3] https://www.imdb.com/title/tt0103241/
[4] https://www.imdb.com/title/tt0101912/

on the bus. I'm the one with the curly hair, chatting with my best friend Blair, who was Garry's Director of Development at the time and is single handedly responsible for me getting both my job with Ziskin and with Marshall. Thanks to that epic role in the movie, I also score an impressive royalty check from SAG every few years for about a dollar and a half.

The two years I spent at Garry's Henderson Productions were amazing. Garry was deceptively brilliant, dropping words of wisdom that I still follow today. Ultimately, though, the pace of features was a tad too slow for me, and I started looking for work back on the TV side. At the time, Fox was expanding from four to seven nights of programming a week, and had a job open in Comedy Development. After landing the gig, I spent the next five years working on *Martin,*[5] *Roc,*[6] and *Ned and Stacy,*[7] and developing half-hours like *Living Single,*[8] *Clueless,*[9] and *The Wild Thornberrys.*[10]

Being a comedy exec suited me. My time as a writer's assistant had given me a solid foundation in what was funny and how to give notes on story and character. I also spent nearly every night out with my friends at the L.A. comedy clubs, so I knew who the up-and-coming talent was on the circuit. And when Tom Nunan, Executive Vice President of Development, eventually left to run development for UPN, I went over with him to take over the comedy department.

---

[5] https://www.imdb.com/title/tt0103488/
[6] https://www.imdb.com/title/tt0101184/
[7] https://www.imdb.com/title/tt0112093/
[8] https://www.imdb.com/title/tt0106056/
[9] https://www.imdb.com/title/tt0115137/
[10] https://www.imdb.com/title/tt0167743/

I spent the next four years developing *Girlfriends,*[11] *The Parkers,*[12] Ryan Reynolds' first sitcom *Two Guys, A Girl, and a Pizza Place*[13] which aired on ABC, and *Malcolm in the Middle*[14] which went to Fox. But as dramas started to rise in popularity and slots for comedies became fewer and farther between, it became clear to me that I needed to broaden my skill set. When UPN asked me to re-up for another stint, I declined, instead partnering up with producer Jonathan Axelrod, who already had a deal with Paramount. In addition to comedy, Jonathan and I branched out into drama and film, and over the six years we were together, were able to sell multiple projects and produce a one hour drama series.

At the network, it's one thing to listen and react to pitches that come in fully formed, but it's an entirely different thing to get into the weeds on a concept with a writer from start to finish. By the time we finally shuttered our production company. I was confident in my ability to switch back and forth from buyer to seller.

The leap into the corporate ranks forced me to stretch my abilities in a different way, and allowed me to step onto a much bigger playing field than I ever imagined. While daunting at first, I discovered the more I said yes to the small asks — moderating panel discussions, creating programs, writing reports — the easier it was to tackle the larger ones like overseeing the diversity council comprised of the heads of all of the major divisions. The job was what I liked to call HR adjacent — close

[11] https://www.imdb.com/title/tt0247102/
[12] https://www.imdb.com/title/tt0200353/
[13] https://www.imdb.com/title/tt0137330/
[14] https://www.imdb.com/title/tt0212671/

enough to see the hiring, retention, promotion, and termination process without having to report into HR directly. This vantage point was illuminating, giving me countless new insights into what gives one candidate the edge over another.

I was eager to get back to a more creative space, so after six years at NBCU, in 2013, when HBO came looking for someone to begin their diversity efforts, it felt like the perfect move. For seven years I created and oversaw HBO's emerging artists programs, fostering the careers of the up-and-coming writers, directors, cinematographers, and crew who came through our doors.

Over the course of my career, I've learned a few valuable things, one of them being that working in this industry is a gift. Where else can you spend all day asking "what if" and get paid for it? Yes, we all have to pay our dues. Most of us weren't born into Hollywood families, so we have to work at generating opportunities for ourselves. But once we do, we find we just aren't built to do anything else. We love creating and sharing those creations with others. We love the magic of storytelling.

However, and this is a big however, your path might not materialize in quite the way you envisioned it. At least, not at first. And that's okay. Be open. You might not ever get on the staff of your favorite sitcom, but you might write a book for Audible. You might have a lucrative career directing movies on a streamer instead of big-budget theatrical features. You might be cast in a long-running drama instead of a comedy. So, keep an open mind and say yes to everything. Remember, until recently Netflix, Apple

TV+, Disney+, Amazon Studios, and HBOMax weren't even a thing. Netflix still delivered DVDs in the mail, and rebranding CBS All Access to Paramount+ wasn't even remotely a concept. If you came to Hollywood only wanting to work at a broadcast network, you would've completely missed every other platform on the verge of taking off.

Before we get started with the nuts and bolts of how we do what we do, here is a little advice. Let go of the fear. You will waste a lot of valuable time worrying about whether or not you will make it in Hollywood. Unless you're actively working against your own best interests, you will succeed. It's not about if, it's about when.

Most writers I know get excited about their work, then spend the rest of their time beating themselves up that it's not good enough. I won't lie. That part of the creative process will not go away. You will definitely have those moments of self-doubt that come with being a creative soul. You'll wallow in imposter syndrome, mentally ripping apart the thing you were so excited about writing just a few minutes ago. You'll think you have no talent. You'll wonder how you ever thought you could write something worthy of being read by anyone other than your mother. After all, shouldn't you be perfect at everything you try, right this very second?

The answer is no, no, and absolutely not. If your work was perfect the first time you put it on paper, there'd be no such thing as notes, revisions, and an amazing little thing called discovery. You'd never seek to go deeper to find new levels of honesty, because when it's a work of sheer genius the first time out, why not quit while you're ahead? Insisting your work be perfect from jump puts an enormous amount of pressure on you too early in the game. You'll wind up quitting before you've even started to pick up steam. Stephen King and JK Rowling received a massive amount of rejection letters before they broke through. But they never gave up. They kept working their craft. Unsurprisingly, King and Rowling are just the tip of the iceberg when it comes to stories like these. Add Sylvester Stallone, Tyler Perry and many more to the list. If these writers had given up, none of us would have ever heard of Andy Dufresne, Harry Potter, Rocky, or Medea. That alone would be tragic.

The point is, getting better takes work, and a tiny bit of doubt that makes you strive to do the best you can do is healthy. Just don't spend time wallowing in misery to the point where it becomes unproductive. Give yourself five minutes a day of "woe is me" whining and then move on. Anything else is a waste of time.

Here's a good exercise to rid yourself of imposter syndrome: think back to when you first saw someone like you on screen and remember how amazing it felt. You were probably a kid at the time and, maybe for the first time, you found yourself excited and comforted that you weren't so weird and alone after all. Now, think of that kid sitting in front of a screen right now, desperate to feel the same way you did — excited, comforted, validated. By bringing yourself to this process, you bring a perspective we don't already have in television, because you are uniquely you. Only you can write the characters and stories we need to see next. You need to be in this game so that someone else can see themselves and know that it's okay to be who they are.

Don't spend your energy imagining what it will be like living in your parents' basement when you're sixty as you futilely try to break into Hollywood. That's almost certainly not going to happen. Show up knowing that it will work out, because it will. You may have to take a regular job until you get on staff or sell that great idea, and that's a good thing. You can't write about life without being immersed in it first. Then bring that experience, and every other experience you've ever had, to your page. Instead of spending that valuable time worrying, spend it creating.

Now let's get to work.

CHAPTER 1

LAYING THE GROUNDWORK

For some reason, television development is one subject they never seem to teach in school. You can sign up for acting, directing, and writing classes, but development remains this mysterious netherworld of coded language and secret handshakes that rarely sees the light of day. And yet, it's one of the most important aspects of the industry. Creative executives are charged with identifying great projects, giving notes, collaborating with producers, managing budgets, overseeing production and post, and dealing with the marketing. All valuable and necessary skills that together push your project toward the finish line.

Otherwise known as the creative process, development involves finding a great concept, then working with the creative team to make sure the script is the best it can be. It's the executive's job to figure out if that story has enough "legs" to be told over multiple seasons. If it does, then the marriage of that idea with a writer who can breathe life into it makes it a package worth buying. Once the idea is sold, it's then shaped based on the buyer's needs, until it's ready to go into production. The project is literally "developed" by the writer and the executive into a finished script.

My path to becoming an executive was a winding road through many different aspects of production and development. It started right out of college, when I assisted a talent manager who had an office in a courtyard at the corner of Poinsettia and Beverly Boulevard in West Hollywood. A buddy from high school asked me to take over his summer job, filling the gap between his exit and the arrival of the permanent assistant, expected to start a month later. I'll be the first to admit, I've never landed a job that wasn't a hook up from a friend, so for me the old saying, "It's not what you know, it's who you know" is one hundred percent true.

My duties were to answer phones, and make sure that the actors knew where their auditions were. As much as I liked to think I had the hang of things, in truth, I was awful at the job and found myself at the receiving end of an angry tirade almost daily. The manager handled a roster of well-known celebrities and popular stand-ups. One afternoon, I forgot to tell one of those stand-ups that he had an audition for an acting role. Even though I finally got word to him and he made it to the appointment late, I knew my days were numbered.

Preemptively, I marched across the courtyard where a casting office aptly called The Casting Company, was hiring. I had every confidence that I would be great at manning their phones and filing headshots for the team. Having already sparked a relationship with the lead assistant, my transition over from the manager's office was seamless. Terrified of repeating my bad performance, I vowed to do better. Little did I realize this small move would be a step toward finding my true passion.

Jane Jenkins and Janet Hirshenson were the go-to casting directors for Francis Ford Coppola, Ron Howard, Rob Reiner, and John Hughes, so I had access to some of the best scripts in town. The mid-80s were pre-email, pre-texting days. Messengers delivered scripts by hand, and they then had to be copied. Sitting at the front desk was the perfect perch for me to receive everything that came in, so when John Hughes' new script *Ferris Bueller's Day Off*[15] came in, it landed right in my hot little hands. Over the next year or so, Jane and Janet would work on *Stand By Me,*[16] *Beetlejuice,*[17] and *The Princess Bride.*[18] I consumed everything I could, and when the other assistant, Jill, asked if I wanted to make a few extra bucks on the side writing coverage for a small production company, I jumped at the chance. Eventually, the casting company hired Denise Chamian as their associate, who introduced me to executive producers Jerry Perzigian and Don Seigel. Don and Jerry had just wrapped the final season of *The Jeffersons,*[19] and were rolling into a deal with Norman Lear's Embassy Productions, housed on the Sunset Gower lot. I had been honing my ability to break down material, and working with comedy writers seemed like it would be right up my alley.

THE EXECUTIVE RANKS

The entertainment industry is based on an apprenticeship model. Candidates are pipelined in from the bottom to learn how to do a job from those more experienced before

---

[15] https://www.imdb.com/title/tt0091042/
[16] https://www.imdb.com/title/tt0092005/
[17] https://www.imdb.com/title/tt0094721/
[18] https://www.imdb.com/title/tt0093779/
[19] https://www.imdb.com/title/tt0072519/

they are ready to assume a more senior role. There's no right way to get in, but once you do, there is a hierarchy in place to ensure that you get the proper training to eventually lead your own team. Simply put, no matter what kind of job you have in the industry, you gain more skills as you move up the ladder.

The entry-level for executives starts at assistant. They're the ones responsible for keeping the exec they are working for on track, on time, and well supplied with all of the tools needed to get through the day. The life's blood of the company, without them, every exec would surely fall apart. I once overheard an assistant joke that as soon as his boss was promoted, she contracted "executive finger," instantly having forgotten how to dial her own phone. These fearless soldiers on the front lines are the gatekeepers to the decision makers, or, in *Ghostbusters'* [20] terms, the valiant Keymaster to their very own Zuul.

The assistant rolls calls, keeps the calendar, accepts material, logs it, and distributes it to the rest of the team. They take notes, make travel plans, enter in the expense reports, schedule breakfast, lunch, dinner, and cocktails, and make sure the exec shows up where they're supposed to. They're also tasked with prioritizing who gets to speak to their boss and when. With not a second of downtime in an exec's day, all callers are definitely not equal. If you've ever wondered why it takes so long to get a call returned in Hollywood, it's because someone more important pushed you further toward the back of the line, and the assistant was the one who made that decision on their boss' behalf.

---

[20] https://www.imdb.com/title/tt0087332/

In return for all of the hand-holding an assistant has to do, the exec shares the vast knowledge of how to survive the industry with their de facto mentee. By listening in on phone calls and notes sessions, and, when lucky enough to be invited into an actual meeting, the assistant starts to understand how things are done.

There's an old adage in Hollywood that cautions, "Be nice to people on your way up because you'll meet them on your way down." That phrase was most definitely coined about an assistant, since it's common knowledge that today's assistants are tomorrow's VPs. Everyone who once sat on someone's desk as an assistant back in the '80s is now running some division of some company somewhere. My former assistants are now Senior VPs and Presidents in their own right. All I can do is hope that I treated them with respect, because they now hold my future in their hands.

These are the levels in the executive ladder. Some companies include an Associate Manager or Executive Director, but those are half-step titles intended to prevent execs from rising too quickly and creating a top-heavy organizational structure.

EXECUTIVE HIERARCHY
Chief Executive Officer
President
Executive Vice President
Senior Vice President
Vice President
Director
Manager
Coordinator
Assistant

One step up from the assistant is the coordinator, whose job is similar to the assistant's, but at this point, they no longer have to answer the phones. As the most junior exec on the creative team, the coordinator compiles competitive information about what's happening in town, writes coverage for scripts, and keeps the database of creative talent. Officially on the executive ladder, they are often tasked with doing the first round of notes that are then handed up to a more senior creative to look over and polish.

Making the move from coordinator to manager can be one of the hardest leaps, primarily because so many of the manager roles were eliminated at many companies, as consolidations and mergers in the 2000s forced severe budget cuts. At one time, ABC and NBC had Associates Training Programs that pipelined promising young talent into their ranks, but those programs created a surplus of junior execs that the companies couldn't always absorb. Without an ROI (return on investment) to show a high conversion rate into permanent hires, instead of downsizing, the networks opted to get rid of the programs altogether. Finding a manager job is still possible, but they aren't nearly as plentiful as they used to be. At some companies, assistants wait for three, four, or even five years before nabbing that elusive promotion.

At the manager level, execs are firmly on their way to a leadership role. Often at the assistant or coordinator level, people are still figuring out what they really want to do within the industry. Some are still deciding whether to pursue writing, and the assistant gig is just a placeholder until they get their chance to roll onto a show. Once someone has reached manager level, they've pretty much decided that the executive path is for them.

Managers do much of the same thing as directors and VPs. Still in the learning stage, they might not have the gravitas to run solo on a project, but they've paid their assistant and coordinator dues and are a trusted member of the team. Agents and lit managers now regularly send them material directly, and the community sees them as someone who can be their "in" to a meeting or a pitch.

As execs are promoted into the upper levels, they gain more and more clout, status, and leverage in moving their projects forward. At the director level, they begin managing junior executives and building critical leadership skills. By VP and SVP, they may even be running their own department. They are now responsible for the direction their development slate takes and are held accountable for its successes and failures.

At the president level, the creative duties start to fall away, and the business of the business begins to take more time and focus. The overall direction of the company, personnel management, marketing, publicity, finance, and sales meetings dominate a president's schedule versus script notes and meetings with talent. For some, the fun of the creative process is gradually replaced with the weighty decisions of running a business. For others, being able to guide a company forward is the ultimate power move.

Like every other creative person in the business, a development executive chooses this path because they love words and storytelling. In order to guide others into creating ideas that resonate emotionally, they have to be fluent in what makes a script great. They need to be knowledgeable about literature, theater, films, and television to build reference points, and they must be able to translate their thoughts succinctly, cogently, and diplomatically to writers. Like everyone else in Hollywood, they are craftsmen who put in the time to be the best that they can be. As pitches come in, they are tasked with assessing whether those concepts work for their needs, and then set about nurturing them into existence as fully realized series.

THE BROADCAST DEVELOPMENT CALENDAR

In the broadcast world, the development cycle officially begins when everyone returns from the July 4th weekend. July, August, and September see the most action when networks are eagerly hearing the pitches they think will work for their audience. By the end of the year, network budgets begin to run dry, slowing the pace down a bit. While drama departments are usually done buying sometime in October, at half the page count and being faster to write, comedy purchasing extends a few weeks later into the fall before buying season officially ends.

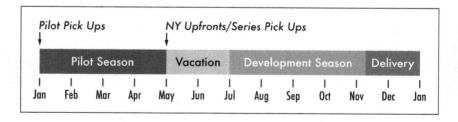

Fig. 1

By Christmas, all scripts are expected in. It gives the network a few precious weeks, when the entire town finally takes some time off, to make a decision about which projects move forward in January after the break. Those who are lucky enough to get a pick-up immediately begin a frantic scramble to produce the pilot in time for a May delivery. Writers who don't get projects picked up go back to the drawing board to get a jump on the upcoming season.

Creating a network schedule requires volume. For every series ordered, many have to go into development. It's hard to tell just what you have until you see it on screen. No one ever knows what's going to work, so it's necessary to buy multiple projects to see which ones make it through successfully. There can be a million little reasons why a project either works or doesn't. To mitigate those factors, networks purchase more ideas than they can possibly air in one year, just to give themselves options. It's the executive's job to shepherd all of them through the development process until they emerge on the other side.

After a new series is ordered in May, the showrunner begins to mount it by hiring the writers for the writer's room while the studio launches into production. So, just as the development exec who helped shepherd the project this far is starting a new pitch season, they are also collaborating with the current executive who will oversee the series moving forward. Working side by side, the two departments ensure there is a smooth transition from development to current (series currently in production) and that nothing is lost in translation. This requires everyone to be in the loop as the network gets ready for a September launch. For all involved, the workload is intense and the pressure high.

CABLE'S YEAR-ROUND SCHEDULE

Because they are subscriber based and not reliant on advertisers, premium cable networks like HBO and Show-time, and basic cable nets such as USA and F/X, have the luxury of airing series whenever they want. Not bound by a fall launch, HBO airs their new series at all times of the year. *Lovecraft Country*[21] enjoyed a mid-August premiere, well ahead of the usual September roll out for the broad-casters. *Game of Thrones*[22] stuck mostly to spring premiere dates, but skipped a year between seasons 7 and 8. *Curb Your Enthusiasm*[23] may have had the most unconventional airing pattern of all, taking years off between seasons 8 and 9 before returning to the schedule in 2017.

Basic cable often prefers to roll out shows in the sum-mer to take advantage of what used to be an open playing field. USA's *Queen of the South*[24] and *Mr. Robot*[25] both pre-miered in June, although by its third season, *Mr. Robot* launched in October. Starz rolled out *Power*[26] in July, the same with *P-Valley,*[27] even though they first aired *Out-lander*[28] in August, and F/X began airing *Fargo*[29] in April but started *Better Things*[30] in September.

---

[21] https://www.imdb.com/title/tt6905686/
[22] https://www.imdb.com/title/tt0944947/
[23] https://www.imdb.com/title/tt0264235/
[24] https://www.imdb.com/title/tt1064899/
[25] https://www.imdb.com/title/tt4158110/
[26] https://www.imdb.com/title/tt3281796/
[27] https://www.imdb.com/title/tt9340526/
[28] https://www.imdb.com/title/tt3006802/
[29] https://www.imdb.com/title/tt2802850/
[30] https://www.imdb.com/title/tt4370596/

Cable also has the ability to develop a show over a longer amount of time. Compared to any comedy on CBS, which would take less than a year to write, be ordered to pilot, and then picked up to series, HBO's *Insecure*[31] took a leisurely three years to develop. Cable projects are ready when they are ready, not when a timetable insists that they be. Due to this flexibility, cable nets don't have to fight for the same dwindling resources in the same short window as the broadcast networks. They can pull the trigger whenever it suits them. Additionally, their lower volume allows them to spend strategically. While the big nets air upward of 200 scripted episodes each year, a cable platform only needs to air a fraction of that amount, the rest of the schedule can consist of acquired movies, sports, documentaries, specials, and alternative programming.

Cable holds one more advantage over the competition — the ability to air shorter orders than broadcast. Only producing eight to thirteen episodes per year, the cable timeline allows for more of the creative process to play out without straining as many production resources.

THE STREAMING REVOLUTION

The advent of streaming platforms has changed viewing patterns significantly. Not straightjacketed by weekly rollouts, being forced to consider schedule flow, or having to search for companion pieces to pair with existing hits, streamers have the flexibility to release their content in whatever way maximizes impact. Whether dropping full seasons all at once, rolling episodes out weekly, or

---

[31] https://www.imdb.com/title/tt5024912/

releasing three episodes at a time, these new platforms make each show its own event.

The upside for the viewer is that they can seek out the content whenever they have the time or the inclination. The downside is that each show must stand on its own, without the support of other shows to prop it up. Without the benefit of a lead-in from a stronger show, a viewer has to find new content via compelling advertising or word of mouth.

Netflix appeals to your particular likes and dislikes using algorithms which select the thumbnail images most likely to get you to watch that show. What you watch tells them what else you are likely to sample. They assume that if you liked the last one, you'll like this next one.

Appealing to what viewers respond to isn't a new concept, but the amount of data the streamers collect allows them to look at their audience in a variety of ways. They can pinpoint exactly when their viewers lose interest, what actors they like, what genres they tend to lean in to, and they know that if they can get the audience to stick with a show until episode three, there's a very high probability that they will finish the show until the end of the season. If the streaming site is connected to a retailer, they can also assume your taste based on your purchasing habits. Such precision helps streamers draw you in, hoping to grab your attention and hold onto it in a vice grip as long as possible.

MEASURING SUCCESS

When DVR'ing moved onto the scene, the traditional ways of tabulating who was watching what programming quickly became antiquated. If audiences were recording their shows and not watching them right away, how could a network possibly be able to tell what was working and what wasn't? Evaluating success now needed to expand to include the date the show aired plus a three to seven-day spread, which was the amount of time research departments were guessing it took for someone to watch the show. Yet another shift happened when that spread went from seven days to thirty, and again when it became evident that it was necessary to capture the cumulative views of an episode which aired multiple times during the week, the streaming platform views, and video on demand. As audiences continue to fracture, counting eyeballs continues to evolve, and attempts to reach viewers grow even more targeted.

Streamers have successfully thrown a grenade into how we now watch television. However, the evolution really started with the VCR boom in the '80s, which allowed us to tape shows and watch them at our leisure. The original DVRs (digital video recorder), TiVo and Replay, made things even easier, as recording no longer required us to use a physical VHS videotape. It made storing content easy, prevented the inevitable scramble to find a usable VHS cassette, and made the horror of taping over your parents' anniversary video a thing of the past. Everything was neatly saved onto the device itself. As audiences began programming their own lineups and watching them at will, schedule flow, companion programming, and commercial breaks flew out the window. With a few taps of the remote, viewers could quickly fast forward over pesky ads. Even though the show still had to air on television before it was able to be recorded, they could still watch what they wanted when they wanted. A power shift from network to consumer was beginning, and the ways in which executives marked success started to evolve.

When I first joined Fox in the early '90s, the Research Department delivered household ratings, which were the numbers and percentages of who was watching what across America. It became clear, however, that those numbers weren't as helpful to a niche network like Fox, and that focusing specifically on how we were doing with our particular audience made much more sense. The sweet spot for Fox was viewers 18–49 years old, and those were the demos they reported. Not interested in being all things to all people, Fox wanted to be known as a destination place for the young, hip set. Hoping to appeal to those interested in more edgy fare, Fox programming pushed the limits of what was typically seen elsewhere.

By the time I moved over to run comedy for UPN in the late '90s, we were even more specific in the audience we pursued. With a focus on an underserved audience, *Girlfriends* and *The Parkers* pulled in great 18–49 numbers. The 12–24 female demos who tuned in for *Moesha*[32] and *Clueless* on Tuesday nights, and the 18–34 male demos that showed up for broader comedies, high concept dramas, and wrestling[33] balanced out our schedule. Knowing who we were programming for, and continuing to meet their needs, became much more important than trying to deliver content to satisfy everyone.

---

[32] https://www.imdb.com/title/tt0115275/
[33] https://en.wikipedia.org/wiki/WWE_SmackDown

CHAPTER 2

THE EXECUTIVE MINDSET

*L*ike you, creative executives grew up entranced by movies and television. And like you, we knew we wanted to be a part of the world that brought those stories to life. We are charged with identifying talented writers, directors, and actors, and packaging them with concepts that an audience will consume ravenously. We're predictors of future trends, guiders of projects, and team leaders rolled into one. We deal with marketing, sales, finance, publicity, internal and external stakeholders, wrangle difficult personalities, and manage up, down, and across the organization chart. It's a tall order.

This is not to whine about the job at all, it's merely to give an overview of the position's scope. And not all execs do everything well. We have our blind spots and our deficiencies, just like in every other business. Execs catch flack for being risk averse. We also tend to get a bad rap for stifling creativity and giving dumb notes. We get it. We've heard the jokes. However, for every awful tale about how some executive almost killed a project, there are just as many examples of those who nurtured a script, and championed it against the odds and into existence.

When mega dollars are at stake, it's critical to know where to place your bets. Not everyone can deliver a quality show on time and on budget, and so much goes into producing a series, it's understandable that an exec would be a little trigger shy. When a show fails, it's months, if not years, of work down the drain. With so many decisions along the way, it's no wonder that for every hit, there are scores of busted pilots lying in their wake.

The head of a major movie studio once told me that for every film they produced, it would cost the same $40M to promote it. It didn't make any difference if the production budget was $5M or $50M, they still needed $40M for marketing. That being the case, he would much rather place his bets on a splashy $50M film, because he had a better chance of recouping his investment than a smaller indie project.

Not quite the same as the movie business; television is still also about taking calculated shots. Launching a new show requires a tremendous financial output, and success is never guaranteed. That accounts for the rise in reboots, spin-offs, an emphasis on working with big names, and packaging. The hope is to take as much of the guesswork as possible out of the equation.

Quite a few factors come into play when we're making decisions about what we buy and what we need to add to our programming lineups, some of it coming from past experiences and conventional wisdom handed down from those who held our seats before we did. That wisdom provides the guardrails that we either work within, or push against, in order to support new ideas that evolve the form.

DEVELOPING FOR TIME SLOTS

Unlike streamers, where everything is available at all times, broadcasters program morning, afternoon, news, prime-time, and late-night dayparts. We look at what's already working on air, assess where our schedule is weakest, and develop a show for that time period. If we don't think the new show is strong enough to anchor a night, we place it in what's called a hammock position between two already successful shows. Sandwiched between popular series, the hope is the newbie will eventually become a hit after the audience has a chance to sample it.

To keep an audience from flipping the channel, series are scheduled with other series the network believes work well together. It's easy to see why procedurals are usually programmed with other procedurals, and shows lighter in tone are paired up with other similarly toned shows. Because hour-longs never start on the half-hour, networks always program two comedies together, requiring every comedy to have a companion piece to go with it. Darker hours will always be programmed in the 10 p.m. slot, when it's assumed that the kids have already gone to bed and the adults can enjoy edgier fare.

When deciding what kind of show to pitch to a network, consider what time slots might be vulnerable and where they might have needs. If they tend to have a robust comedy lineup, you might have a shot at selling them a half-hour if it works with their profile. But if they only program one hour of comedy per week and both slots are taken by high-performing hits by one particular producer, you might be better off looking elsewhere.

DEVELOPING BY GENRE

Developing by genre involves looking at the white space to see what's not on the air, and then trying to fill it with what's missing. If audiences are enjoying our family dramas, we develop more family dramas. If physical comedies see a ratings bump, we'll put more into development so that we can build on our momentum. We assess what's currently working and try to replicate that success by providing more of the same to an enthusiastic audience. In fact, developing by genre is such a good organizer of content that the Syfy channel broke off an entire category, all for one rabid and loyal audience.

If a particular kind of show hasn't been on air in a while, it might be time to reinvent the genre for a new generation. Staple genres like police procedurals, medical dramas, and legal franchises can always be found on air, but they might not always appear in great quantities. For a while hospital shows were scarce, until *ER*[34] burst on the scene with its multiple-storylines, chaotic pacing, and technical jargon reimagining the form.

Other genres had similar resurgences. When superhero movies burst back on the big screen, they also found a home on the small one. But before they regained popularity in theaters, there were few to none on TV. Prior to *The Sopranos*[35] launch, no network would have even considered a show about mobsters, believing a show about unlikeable characters would never work. Before *West Wing*,[36] it was impossible to air a show about politics. Back

---

[34] https://www.imdb.com/title/tt0108757/
[35] https://www.imdb.com/title/tt0141842/
[36] https://www.imdb.com/title/tt0200276/

in 2000, drama was dead, and comedy was king. This was all conventional wisdom for the time, proving that it is what it professed to be — conventional.

Of course, there are good reasons why certain kinds of shows haven't worked well historically. For instance, it's incredibly hard to do a comedy about God. While spiritual shows may work in an hour format, getting anyone to pony up dollars for something that pokes fun at such a sacred topic is nearly impossible. So, if taking that on is your jam, just know that you may have fewer places to sell it.

Before *American Horror Story* [37] and shows like it brought back the anthology format, you couldn't pitch one without someone shaking their head and telling you that they would never buy one at their network. Execs will tell you that audiences come back each week to see the recurring characters they've fallen in love with, while anthology series rely on new characters appearing in each episode.

Even though they still aren't developed in large quantities, we are seeing more anthologies than in the past. *AHS* managed to give us both recurring casts, if only for a season at a time, and new situations from year to year. More along the lines of a limited series than a true anthology, it's created a new model for us to enjoy.

Wonder why we don't see more romantic comedies on TV? Executives don't just shy away from this type of show, they head for the hills when one is pitched. Conventional wisdom says they simply don't work. As much as audiences have clamored for another *Moonlighting*, [38] resting

---

[37] https://www.imdb.com/title/tt1844624/
[38] https://www.imdb.com/title/tt0088571/

an entire series on the chemistry between two actors is a disaster in the making. Heaven forbid one of the two stars opts out of the show at any point. And even if they stick it out for the full run, the endless waiting to see "will they or won't they" quickly exhausts an audience's patience.

The only way a romantic comedy (or "rom/com") can survive is if it is first built on a solid foundation and the romance becomes the added interest on top. Fox's *Bones*[39] laced a romantic comedy through a cop show about forensic anthropology. While the mystery of the week held the show up, Bones and Booth falling in love was the juicy, gooey center that kept us hooked.

Keeping a good mix of genres on the air also prevents a network from ignoring an underserved audience. Too many of one kind of show signals it might be worth expanding to other concepts.

CHASING DEMOS

Ever since Colgate started selling toothpaste and soap suds to housewives, its goal was to capture the attention of the female in the house, who bought the household essentials. Those women were loyal customers who, once they found a brand they liked, usually stuck with it. They controlled the purse strings on daily purchases, accounting for most of the household's disposable income. Big ticket items like washing machines and refrigerators were marketed to wives, while automobiles were marketed to their husbands. Old fashioned thinking for sure, but where

---

[39] https://www.imdb.com/title/tt0460627/

the advertising dollars were concerned, this was a proven strategy.

By the time I got to Fox, advertisers in general were chasing college educated young "upscale" white viewers, valuing them over the "urban" black audience. Consumers from major metropolitan areas known as A and B counties were more desirable than rural C and D counties.

At a certain point, somewhere around the mid-'90s, there was a new push to develop toward a demographic (also known as a "demo") that had always proven hard to wrangle, the 18–34 year old male. Pulling in this elusive group had never been easy. Easily distracted by video games, sporting events, concerts, and hanging out with friends on the weekends, this group became "the one that got away," the advertiser's holy grail. Programming for the young man in the house eventually became the goal. Male leads became more prevalent than female ones, and each year more and more male-skewing programming was developed.

History had shown us, however, that female-skewing shows were just as valuable, if not more so. Women have always driven big ratings. Shows like *Designing Women,* [40] *The Golden Girls,* [41] and *Murphy Brown* [42] were juggernaut hits with strong female characters taking center stage, and even shows like *Frasier,* [43] *Cheers,* [44] and *Wings* [45] catered to women by featuring romantic storylines.

---

[40] https://www.imdb.com/title/tt0090418/
[41] https://www.imdb.com/title/tt0088526/
[42] https://www.imdb.com/title/tt0094514/
[43] https://www.imdb.com/title/tt0106004/
[44] https://www.imdb.com/title/tt0083399/
[45] https://www.imdb.com/title/tt0098948/

Knowing who you are developing content for is key. Because we know who is watching what by virtue of the ratings they garner, we can make generalizations about what else they will like. The age of the star customarily determines the age of the show's audience. The younger the lead, the more likely it will attract a younger demo. Women love mysteries, soapy dramas, and relationship comedies, men gravitate toward cop shows, sports, and action.

As a writer, demos are important because you have to know what audience you are writing for. The same audience that watches procedurals on CBS is not the same group that will show up for *PEN15*.[46] Have a clear idea who might be interested in watching your show so you can make your case for why an exec should say yes.

TASTE CLUSTERS

Netflix looks at something called "taste clusters" as a way to group subscribers interested in a particular kind of programming. With so much data at their fingertips, they may notice that a certain segment of their audience gravitates toward a particular group of shows. They can then take that information and develop to fill that audience's desire for more shows like what they've already confirmed they like.

Taste clusters aren't demos which target large groups of viewers by age, race, gender, or location. They aren't genre categories used to identify a certain type of show. Clusters are the fans themselves, who like certain types of

---

[46] https://www.imdb.com/title/tt8324422/

content or certain aspects of shows. Those fans might love broad comedies, action rom/coms, or psychological thrillers. They might watch content starring a specific actor, or some other targeted element. The common denominator might cut also across all demos. As they rally around the content they love, they become prime targets for more shows to be developed specifically for them.

This new way of looking at viewers also exists at similar platforms. At Amazon Studios they call these groupings "audience segments." However, as Netflix and the other streamers perfect how they use their data to develop content, the concept of taste clusters may eventually drift off into the ether. Things are happening so fast in the streaming universe it's very possible that today's terminology will be out of date tomorrow.

What will never change, however, are the ways buyers look to serve their audiences and give them more of what they clamor for.

CHAPTER 3

GETTING IN

*E*very person in Hollywood has an opinion about how to break into the industry. Nine times out of ten, those opinions are based on their own experiences. After all, if it worked for them, it should work for everyone, right? Truth be told, there is no one right way. Some people wedge their way in through an agency mailroom, while others enter through the production door, college internship, or if you're lucky enough to win the gene-pool lottery, good old-fashioned nepotism. Inroads to a career in entertainment are endless. Even if you don't have a clear idea about where you want to end up, just getting in is the first step. And it all boils down to one thing: relationships.

Let's face it, people want to work with people they know, and it's much easier to go with a known factor than it is to take the risk with someone from the outside. We hedge our bets by hiring those in close proximity to us. It's not a perfect science. In fact, it can lead to a vast number of great candidates being overlooked because they aren't immediately on our radar. Never allowing new people outside of our bubble to enter into our friend group means always hiring people who think the same and have similar ideas. And if we've learned nothing else from *The Matrix,*[47] we know that generating more Agent Smiths is never a good thing. But things happen quickly in Hollywood, and what's easiest usually wins.

BY THE TIME YOU'VE APPLIED, THE JOB IS ALREADY GONE

You see a job listed on a company's website and you apply, but don't get an interview. Why not? Because the job was already gone by the time you hit submit.

By law, HR (Human Resources) is obligated to post every job they have available. But remember when I told you it's about who you know? Weeks ago, when the hiring manager knew that there was a job opening, they started calling everyone they knew to ask who they should hire to fill it. In effect, that job was already gone. It was likely filled long before it showed up online. Whoever was in serious contention was asked to fill an application online, but that is only to ensure that HR has them in the system and can track that they officially applied.

I have heard from friends that they have randomly submitted their resume to HR for a job and been hired, but frankly, those are the exceptions, not the rule, and when pressed about the details, there is always an asterisk involved. For one exec who is now at a large production company, when I probed just a little deeper, she recalled that she had met the hiring manager weeks before she landed the job. At some point, an introduction was made.

---

[47] https://www.imdb.com/title/tt0133093/

USE KEYWORDS

When Conan O'Brien's show moved from New York to L.A., NBC HR posted a job for a production assistant. Within a matter of hours, hundreds of resumes poured in. There was physically no way for the HR manager to look at each and every one, so they searched the applications and resumes for keywords — the same keywords they used in the job posting.

Take a cue directly from the horse's mouth. If whoever is hiring is looking for someone with 5+ years experience, and you have those 5+ years in your background, type 5+ years on your resume. If they want someone with production experience, coding proficiency, or a sales background, bring those skills to the forefront.

Better yet, have someone you know at the company mention to an HR executive that you have applied so your resume can be pulled from the pile and specifically reviewed. It might not get you the job, but it might get your name noticed this time so that you are remembered the next time. I've always said, it takes the first time they meet you for them to bring you back a second time.

Since my job at NBCUniversal included recruiting, I would ask a senior-level executive at one of the networks I oversaw to take five meetings with new potential hires they did not previously know. It was a no-pressure meet and greet, just to get to know great people who were out there, even though we knew there wasn't a job opening. The point was to create relationships early, so that when a job did open up, the senior exec already had someone in mind.

And it worked.

Time and again, the executives I had brought in landed jobs within a year of their first meeting. And because I had introduced more than one at a time, the senior exec had options. It was their choice whom to hire. At that point, it was no longer my idea that they hired any of the candidates, it was theirs.

USE WHAT MAKES YOU SPECIAL

If your resume is filled with jobs in retail, convincing an industry insider that you know how to prioritize their phone sheet better than someone who already knows the town can be a challenge. But it's not insurmountable.

You just need to demonstrate that you've had a track record of being as committed to content as we are. Start with reworking your resume to include your transferable skills. If you've supported multiple bosses at one time, fielded a high volume of calls, have great computer or organizing skills, include that info. Also add in any remotely related special interests, clubs, or awards indicating what you're passionate about. Does your website reviewing the top TV shows of the season have a following? Put it on your resume. If you've taken relevant courses, worked at a theater, volunteered for a festival, or worked production on short films, use it to tell a story about your determination to be a part of the industry. The by-product of engaging in any extracurriculars like these is that they also widen your peer group exponentially. Every classmate, fellow PA, and festival co-worker is a potential connection who is also excited about storytelling. As your resume grows, and your network grows, so do your opportunities.

At NBCUniversal, I was part of the team that sourced and reviewed candidates for our Associate's program, which brought emerging execs into the fold. The ones who stood out were ones who knew what set them apart from the rest of the pack. One interviewee in particular noted that he was a comic book buff. Another, that she was very involved in LGBT organizations. Another indicated that she loved surfing YouTube channels for interesting filmmakers. Whether you're into romance novels, are an avid theatergoer, or watch reality TV, whatever your passion is, make sure you use it to brand yourself.

A background in another field can also be a bonus. Say you've spent the last few years as a lawyer, and you're ready to make a move into television. Every night for the past five years, you've quietly written scripts now piled up in your bottom drawer. You know you can do this, but how?

Whether you know it or not, your experience is an asset. Use it and write what you know. The *Law and Order*[48] franchise has employed multiple lawyers. Amazon's *Jack Ryan*[49] uses a former CIA operative-turned-writer to maintain accuracy. If you're in tech or marketing, write about that. Your specialty immediately sets you apart from the pack, so use it to your advantage by writing a script that highlights your knowledge in that field.

Make it easy for Hollywood to say yes to you by using every bit of ammo at your disposal.

---

[48] https://www.imdb.com/title/tt0203259/
[49] https://www.imdb.com/title/tt5057054/

INTERNSHIPS

Unlike the days when students worked summers for college credit, we're now in a new age in which all of the major studios and networks provide paid internships year-round. Applications are sourced for the fall, spring, and summer terms, but you have to get a jump on them early. These are coveted entry-level positions designed to help you gain experience, add to your resume, and build lasting friendships that will help you secure a job after graduation.

The first stop should be your college career counseling department. In many cases, it already has a long-standing alliance with studios, networks, and production companies. Some companies may need you to be at least a rising sophomore in a four-year institution with a particular GPA to qualify, but smaller places might have fewer restrictions. A quick check of the company's website can suss out the requirements.

Emma Bowen, T. Howard, and The American Black Film Festival provide internships for students of color; their history within the industry and stellar reputations immediately boost your profile simply by association. The Academy of Television Arts and Sciences and the Academy of Motion Picture Arts and Sciences both have internships, as do the L.A. and N.Y. Mayor's Offices. If moving to one of those cities isn't in the cards at the moment, try interning at a local theater, comedy club, or with a writer or director. Your goal is getting that first creative credit on your resume that you can build on to tell a story about how much you love entertainment.

Of course, once you've started your internship, don't let the opportunity in front of you slip by. Do your job to the best of your ability, so that you'll have a stellar recommendation to use when you apply for your next job.

On my first day at HBO, an intern from another department graciously offered to escort me to a meeting. As we were walking the halls, he introduced himself and said that if I needed anything, he'd be happy to help out. I was brand new and didn't want to step on anyone's toes, after all, he supported another exec. But the next day, he asked again. "Hey, if you need anything. . . ."

The following week, my manpower shortage was catching up with me, so I finally took him up on his offer, handing him an assignment that would have taken me days to do. The next day, the finished report appeared in my inbox. It was so perfectly done, I thought for certain he recruited an army of assistants to help out. "Nope," he said. "I handled it on my own." He was ex-military, used to hard work and discipline. Wherever he got his drive, I was impressed, and when his internship was over, I hired him right away.

Stepping up and saying yes to every assignment, no matter how small, works because when you're willing to go the extra mile, people notice. The work you do still has to be good, and people still have to like being around you, but when they know they can rely on you, they will. I also observed plenty of interns who simply sat quietly and waited for someone to hand them an assignment. Those people never went on to full-time jobs.

Another small piece of advice: while you have your internship, get to know as many people as you can. Don't be shy about asking an exec for ten minutes of their time. At this point, your goal is not to get a job, you already have the internship. You just want to hear about what they do and how they got there. This puts you squarely on their radar, so that when something comes up in the future, they already have you in mind.

If you're worried about how to reach out to make the ask, approach your supervisor to make the intro. If you aren't certain they'll help, ask someone else in the department. You can even enlist the receptionist as your ally. The person at the front desk knows everyone in the building. They take the calls and greet every guest who enters through the front door. Establish a relationship with that person, and when appropriate, ask their advice on next steps.

If you're at all concerned about protocol, ask your supervisor or HR rep how to go about it. Chances are, they will be happy to make the intro for you. HR has a vested interest in transitioning you into a full-time employee to boost their conversion rate. They've spent time and money teaching you how the company operates, and would prefer to keep you, rather than to hand that investment over to a competitor.

AGENCIES

Starting in the mailroom may not seem to be the most glamorous move, but working at an agency is a crash course in the hows, whats, and who's who of Hollywood.

There are a handful of large agencies, another handful of medium sized agencies, and a smattering of smaller ones that all offer a way into the business through their entry-levels. A quick web search can turn up an exhaustive list of names and contact information. Odds are good they are looking to hire. But even at the lowest rung on the totem pole, these are insanely competitive positions.

This is a high-stress, high-stakes environment that forces you to be on your game at all times. A year or two on an agent's desk will provide you with valuable relationships that will last your entire career. Temp assignments help you establish a track record inside the industry, make connections, and get a glimpse inside of a particular department so you can decide for yourself if it's something you'd ultimately like to pursue. You'll understand the business from the inside out, and see the various ways that agencies make money for the talent they work with.

The best way to get in is knowing someone who knows someone. Agencies have high turnover rates, so they're always looking for new blood. Many temp jobs turn into permanent ones, so never underestimate the value of a short-term gig. If you can connect with an HR recruiter, ask for a general meeting. It will immediately put you on their radar for future opportunities. Better yet, get to know an assistant who will already be connected to a vast network of their peers who post openings on the agency job boards as soon as a position is open.

Working on this side of the business isn't for everyone. You must come equipped with a thick skin and a willingness to stick it out. Rest assured, you'll be subjected to long hours and low wages, but when you've paid your dues at the bottom, there's nowhere else to go but up.

JOIN AN ORGANIZATION AND VOLUNTEER

When you don't have prior experience, you can get it by volunteering. Not only does volunteering put something on your resume, but it also takes the edge off of entering a new situation alone. When you have a job to do, it's so much easier to connect with others. By handing out badges at a festival, you'll get to see films and you'll have an organic conversation opener when meeting people.

The industry is chock full of organizations that cater to a variety of interests and provide various kinds of support. The Hollywood Radio & Television Society (HRTS) and its offshoot for younger members, the JHRTS, hold panels, as do the ATAS (Academy of Television Arts and Sciences), The Academy of Motion Picture Arts and Sciences, National Association for Multi-ethnicity in Communications (NAMIC), National Association of Latino Independent Producers (NALIP), and the Coalition of Asian Pacifics in Entertainment (CAPE). The DGA, WGA, and PGA offer screenings and skill-building events as well.

Younger folks interested in production have additional pathways available to them through programs like Hollywood CPR, The Ghetto Film School, Inner-City Filmmakers, Streetlights, Manifest Works, Evolve, and Made in NY. These organizations are just the tip of the iceberg when it comes to industry entry-points. Any and every chance to access information and to make contacts is a step in the right direction.

Kelly Edwards with Garry Marshall and Blair Richwood

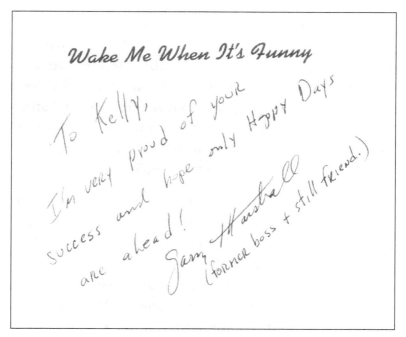

Note from Garry Marshall to Kelly Edwards

CHAPTER 4

LET'S DO LUNCH

*I*ndustry players do breakfast, dinner, and drinks, but what we're known best for is "doing lunch." Sitting down with someone over a friendly meal is our way of kicking off a working relationship. Chatting about our families, where we grew up, and where we went to college greases the wheels for what's about to come — finding ways for us to do business together. Over lunch, we discover each other's career goals, preferred tastes in material, our company mandates, and, most importantly, how we can help fill them.

In many ways, the entertainment industry operates like a small town. After years in the business, you realize you know just about everyone in the neighborhood. People I "did lunch" with when I first started as an executive are the same people I still connect with today. We friend and follow each other on social media, we all attend the same holiday parties, the same screenings, and the same award shows. We've literally grown up with one another. Once you've done lunch with someone, reaching out to them to sell a project or get inside information isn't as difficult as making a cold call to someone you've never met.

The unfortunate thing about lunch dates, however, is they are often canceled. Particularly if the meal is with someone higher up the food chain than you are and something more important suddenly comes up that takes precedence. Putting out fires surpasses introductory lunches every time. But that doesn't mean you should give up the fight to reschedule it again. When I was a mid-level exec, I boldly called the head of Sony Television, who graciously accepted my lunch invitation and then proceeded to reschedule it five times. I knew it wasn't personal. He was three rungs above me and busy running an entire division, and while he was perfectly nice to me whenever we met, I understood that I wasn't his highest priority. I also knew that if I just stayed on his phone sheet, eventually he would feel so guilty about canceling he'd have to keep the lunch. When he finally did, it was well worth the wait. It was a terrific hour and a half which formed a deeper alliance, putting me on more equal ground with him than I'd ever had before.

Not all cancelations result in a happy ending. Some just disappear, never to be put back on the books at all. I've had plenty of lunches I had looked forward to never occur. At a certain point, not rescheduling becomes my personal power move, and the best way to retain my sanity.

LOCATION, LOCATION, LOCATION

When reaching out to someone for breakfast, lunch, dinner, or coffee, make it easy for them to say yes. Pick a venue close to where they are. For breakfast, choose someplace in their part of town, so that it's on the way into their office. If it's lunch, offer to come to them. No one wants to get caught in traffic and, if by some miracle, they do agree to leave their immediate vicinity, by the time they get to wher- ever you are, they will most certainly be annoyed by the commute and the lack of parking. Even if none of it was your fault, you'll spend the first precious minutes recount- ing their awful drive, so it's best just to avoid the trouble altogether. A good rule of thumb is, if their schedule is bus- ier than yours, you do the accommodating. Their assistant will know their favorite place to eat, so listen wisely.

Whatever meal you "do," every exec has his or her favorite watering hole, so ask them where they would like to meet up and then arrive early. If you're meeting for coffee, scope out a table early. If it's lunch, be seated by the time they get there. Avoid the "is our table ready yet" awkwardness if possible so you can get down to business.

Another option is to get creative. After I scored my first TV executive job working at Fox, I asked then Presi- dent, Peter Chernin, to breakfast. But instead of expecting him to take time from his schedule to meet me at a res- taurant, I offered to meet him at his office at 7 a.m. with a box of donuts. Both Chernin and his assistant appreci- ated that I was being respectful of his time. He was used to getting into the office early anyway, and this allowed him to continue to work once we were done. Not only was it a great meeting, but the entire hour we were together went uninterrupted.

FOLLOWING UP

Probably the most important part of establishing your net- work is your ability to follow up after you've made that initial introduction. Most people I know have a hard time staying in touch once the door to a relationship has been wedged open. It's awkward to reach out when you think you have nothing of value to say. Won't it just come off as annoying? Don't they have more important things to do than to answer my silly email?

Just like standing at the hors d'oeuvres station waiting for the chance to spark up a conversation with someone at random, staying on an exec's radar without seeming to only be in it for what they can do for you can be equally as painful. So, what do you do? You make it personal.

Hopefully, after you met with the exec, you wrote down notes reminding you what you discussed. Maybe you connected over where you last vacationed, or how many kids they have and what sports they play. Perhaps you shared the same birth month or talked about a show you both loved or hated. If there was a moment you felt you really clicked, now is the time to use it. Remind them why they liked you by shooting over an email reinforcing that connection.

When I interviewed for the manager job at Fox, I'd connected with Tom over our knowledge of stand-up comics. A few days later, as I was flipping through an entertainment magazine, I found one of Jeff Foxworthy's *You Might Be a Redneck If. . .* lists and sent it to him. He sent back a thanks, saying that it gave him a good laugh. I have no idea if that helped my chances of landing the job, but I do know that little extra point of contact kept me on top of his mind.

Let's tally this up. If an exec is hearing a pitch every hour on the hour, that's around eight pitches per day, five times a week, multiplied on average by three meeting attendees per pitch. That's roughly 120 people per week that the exec comes into contact with. Some will, of course, be people they already know, and a few will be general meetings with only one person, but even if you round that number down considerably, it's still a lot of faces to get to know. Standing out doesn't mean oversharing every little thing about your life, nor does it mean probing into an exec's life to the point where they consider calling security on you, but if you have a genuine connection with them, use it to form a deeper attachment.

The most memorable meetings I've had were ones in which we forgot about the time and simply enjoyed each other's company. The most awkward ones were when someone brought in a paper and pen and asked me questions as though I were the subject of their school newspaper article.

When the meeting is winding down, if you can find an organic way to ask, exchange contact information with them. If someone has set up the meeting for you, they would have made the connection and might have arranged the time and place to meet. If that's the case, you won't have the exec's email or phone number to follow up directly. Every exec has a stack of business cards gathering dust in their drawer so ask them for one. They may give you their assistant's information, which is perfectly okay. Don't take that as a personal affront. They've just given you the contact information for The Keymaster.

REACHING OUT

Never text an executive you don't know well. It's unprofessional.

Even if all of your friends only communicate by text and you've only ever Instagrammed and Tik Tok'd in your life and never seen an actual Gmail account, never use text to communicate with an executive with whom you want to work.

At a certain point, your relationship may graduate from acquaintance to friend or into a working relationship. At that point, you have leaped into a more familiar level and texting will be okay.

The most effective way to follow up with someone you've met is going to be by phoning and emailing. I usually do both for a few reasons — it gives me two points of contact with whomever I'm trying to reach. Calling signals that I'm not afraid to have a conversation on the phone, a big plus particularly for people over a certain age. We grew up having to make those terrible cold calls to land our first jobs, so we carry a bit of "if I had to do it, they should, too" attitude. We also recognize that the world has changed, and that email and texting is the language of those coming up behind us now and, on some unconscious level, we resist it as being less professional. So, for those of us in the exec chairs, if you're afraid to speak to someone on the phone, that's a red flag. Business is still done primarily through calls, and if you can't speak to someone via phone, there's someone else in line behind you who can.

I usually call and if I don't get through, I leave word that I'm going to follow up with an email. That gives the receiver a head's up that I'm going to reach out a second way and it's their preference how to return. I'm also now on their phone sheet and in their email box, so they're seeing my name twice. One way or another, they will get back to me without it seeming forced or demanding. I've just courteously connected twice.

Emailing alone puts the emphasis on following up on the other person, which can be off-putting. There's an underlying presumption in an email that once you have sent it, the ball is in the other person's court and your job is done. "Well, I emailed you. Didn't you get it?" It assumes that we must now reply to you. But for an executive who is already working at top speed to clear their inbox, returning your email may not always be on their to-do list. Especially when someone uses phrases like, "Please let me know." When you send something that implies the responsibility is on us, you have just made it our job to follow up with you and keep you in mind rather than you keeping yourself on our radar. We aren't the ones looking for the opportunity, you are. A better tactic would be for you to say you will follow up with a call in a few days to check in.

One thing most people don't know is that, after blackmailers threatened to release Sony's sensitive company emails in 2014 (many of which were posted on social media), each of the studios imposed limits on how long an email will remain available in an inbox. If they're not archived or saved within 30 to 45 days, they magically disappear into the atmosphere. This means, when you send an email to an exec, if we haven't replied to you within those 30 days, or saved your email, we won't be able to search for you when that perfect job opportunity comes along. Pinging us every so often keeps you on top of our mind. The trick is to do it enough to stay on our radar without becoming a nuisance we never want to hear from again. It's a fine line, and a good rule of thumb is to reach out judiciously. Your email is a reminder that we need to do something — read your material, check out your website, make a call on your behalf — so do it in an upbeat and non-insistent manner, then back off and ping us again every few months with an update on how things are going with your career. When we see you're making progress on your own, we're more apt to reply.

One more practical tip: make your email address your name. When I type in your name, your email address should immediately pop up. Otherwise, I'll have to search my memory bank for what clever email you created when you were in college that everyone thought was hilarious at the time. I'll never remember it, and instead will email the person whose name auto-populates when I type it into the To: field.

Are there exceptions? Sure. But there are many more examples of not having your name in your email working against you than there are of them working for you. Eventually, you might abandon the writesfunny97623 or partyon1978 address, but you probably won't give up the email with your name in it and, as noted before, the plan is for you to be in this industry for a while. Make it easy on everyone and stick to something we can all remember.

SHARING CONTACT INFO

I stopped carrying business cards years ago. I found that I was always losing the ones that other people gave me and never seemed to have enough of my own on hand. Only so many of them fit into those little holders anyway, and if I kept them in my pocket they'd just wind up with dull and dirty edges and not anything I'd feel comfortable handing out as my calling card. Instead, I have my professional contact info loaded into my phone and ready to go. All I have to do is hit share contact with my new bestie. When I send the text to them, I include where we met and maybe something that reminds us about our encounter. And since I now have their phone number in my cell, I add the same info about them. That way, when I search for the event, their name pops up right away. I also try to include a little description of them, since meeting someone once doesn't always cement them in my brain for all eternity. It can be as detailed as what we spoke about or as simple as "girl with interesting blue necklace."

Not everyone will be eager to share their info and will prefer for you to give them a business card or they'll give you theirs. Either way, make sure you are prepared. Sometimes it takes a few points of contact to truly establish a relationship.

WORKING THE ROOM

Here's a Hollywood secret: no one likes networking. It's awkward and scary. We would all rather be home scrolling through Netflix than risk being the only person at the party without someone to talk to. Now that you know that we all feel the same way about having to attend a function in order to advance our careers, let your embarrassment go and figure out how to work a room, because that first meeting might not be in an office or on a Zoom call, it might be at an event.

My ex-husband still takes me to his show's wrap parties, because he knows I will chat someone up at the drop of a hat. But that's far from how I started in this business. I was a painfully shy teenager, who could barely order an ice cream cone at the local Baskin-Robbins. And that was ice cream! Imagine how petrified I had to be to forgo a scoop of peanut butter and chocolate on a sugar cone.

And yet, at a certain point in my life, I asked myself how was the terror I was imagining in my head serving me? All it did was prevent me from doing the things I wanted to do. Sitting in meetings I would mumble brilliant statements under my breath, afraid to utter them out loud while someone bolder spoke up and said the very thing I was thinking. After a while, I realized that the epic fails I was sure I would undoubtedly suffer never actually happened. The worry was worse than the thing itself. I'd worked myself up into a frenzy, certain that I was going to look like an idiot in front of someone who mattered. When that didn't come to pass, I discovered I'd spent valuable time running disaster scenarios in my head, when I could have been doing something truly productive.

It dawned on me that if I was going to make it in Hollywood, I'd have to get over myself and learn how to network. I started watching the crowd for an in and, lo and behold, quite to my surprise, there were loads of other awkward attendees anxiously hovering over the appetizers, trying to strike up a conversation. So now I make the first move. I find someone who looks like they're alone and like a heat-seeking missile, I walk up and say hi. Most times they let out a relieved sigh that someone is talking to them. And frankly, so do I.

Another useful tactic is to take a friend. I've been known to make a great wingman because I'm interested in other people's stories. I didn't learn to be that way on my own. Remember that producer I worked with when I was starting out? Jerry was as comfortable talking to someone he met sitting at a bus stop as he was to the head of a network. Why? Because his philosophy was that everyone has a story worthy of being its own movie. Jerry is infinitely fascinated by each person he comes across, and it's this inquisitiveness that allows him to make friends at the drop of a hat.

Find a Jerry to go with you. That person has to be committed to working the room as a team. He can't go off and leave you hanging. Even though no one likes networking, some people are more people-people than other people. Get that person to be your plus-one.

One more tip for panel Q & As. If you're brave enough, be the first to raise your hand to ask a question. Here's why it's a good move: people always remember the one who asked the first question.

There's always an agonizing silence just as Q & A starts rolling. You know the moment — the painful lull when no one wants to be the first to say something. As frightening as it might seem, that uncomfortable sixty seconds is your time to shine. When everyone around you is looking down at their fingernails because nothing intelligent is coming into their heads, shoot your hand up. Keep it up as the volunteer with the mic maneuvers their way over to you.

On stage, the panelists are quietly thanking you under their breath for making an awkward moment less awkward, and everyone in the audience is breathing a sigh of relief that they are off the hook. They don't have to fill the void by speaking first.

Keep your question short, and don't make it about you. This is not the time to recount how you originally came to town to pursue acting but couldn't book a job, so you became a writer. No one wants to hear that. Ask something relevant to the subject at hand.

If you don't have a brilliant question on the tip of your tongue, simply ask them to clarify a certain point. Ask them to repeat something so that everyone can understand it better. It doesn't matter if you could recite it back to them word for word already. When they answer, nod enthusiastically as if you asked for the benefit of the room. Believe me, you don't have to be Einstein to sound like a genius.

Afterward, you will be a someone that everyone remembers. You are now a friendly face they recognize. They might say they appreciated whatever issue you raised. They may also simply remember you because you were the first one brave enough to save the day.

DRESS THE PART

A few years back, a new intern came into my office at HBO wearing a very spiffy three-piece suit and tie. We had a great meeting and at the end of it, I gave him some advice: ditch the suit for more casual attire and wear what everyone else was wearing. In this day and age, you should definitely feel free to be who you want to be and wear what you want to wear. Just know that what you put on is also telling a story about you.

HBO's unofficial dress code was much more laid back than that — these were jeans-wearing people. Even the head of HR could be seen sporting a sweatshirt from time to time. Every Friday, employees wore HBO branded t-shirts. The suit would have highlighted that he wasn't reading the room.

You don't have to become someone you're not, just at least be aware that what you wear makes a statement about who you are.

Not long ago, I hosted a group of students from an out-of-town university. During a lively discussion about the industry, I had connected with one young woman in particular who was interested in post-production. Afterwards, as the group was exiting the building, one of our post execs wandered by. I called her over to introduce her to my new unofficial mentee, but as they started talking, I looked down to see the student was wearing a pair of leopard print house slippers. My heart sank. She hadn't even taken the time to put on a regular pair of shoes.

In general, Hollywood is a very relaxed town. We don't look like bankers, opting instead for clothes one step up from what you'd wear at a barbeque. There's no need to make getting dressed for a meeting or a pitch a national crisis. No special MI-6 recon is involved. *The Marvelous Mrs. Maisel*[50] creator Amy Sherman-Palladino loves wearing hats. It's her signature style and she wears them well.

My only advice here is to know the culture and make a conscious decision of how you want to show up. And whether it makes sense for you to wear some real shoes.

MEETING EXECUTIVES IN THE WILD

You're standing in a queue of twenty other people eager to speak to a panelist who just stepped off the dais. The panelist edges toward the door. The line moves with her. Every few seconds, you get a few feet closer. You have to use your shoulder to block out the person trying to cut in line. Finally, it's your turn.

If you've ever been to an event where someone you've been dying to meet is speaking, you might get lucky enough to grab a few brief moments with them. When you get your shot, make it count. Have your 20 second networking spiel ready to go. Keep your question brief.

I love attending panels because I often find talent before the rest of the town. I've met quite a few rock star writers and directors well ahead of my peers just by showing up and being a part of the activities. The most successful post-panel conversations I've had have been with people who offer a reason for me to follow up with

---

[50] https://www.imdb.com/title/tt5788792/

them. I'm more inclined to want to connect later with someone who has something to offer in return for my time. Those attendees who have a book, a list, or a website to share based on my needs, are much more interesting than folks simply making an ask. I might give you my assistant's info to save my inbox from being inundated, but it's still an in.

Not all execs find value in panels the way I do. If you find yourself getting the brush off, don't take it too seriously. Public speaking is not in everyone's comfort zone, and you may be rolling up on someone dealing with their own anxieties which have nothing to do with you.

For the most part, though, execs hang around afterward to answer your questions because they want to be helpful. They've already opened the door to a conversation. Be respectful. Don't dominate their time. If you do, you will be dismissed out of hand, because you won't have passed the crazy check.

PASSING THE CRAZY CHECK

Yes, it's a real thing. Before we recommend you to be hired onto a staff, put you in a program, or introduce you to a contact of ours, we need to know that you can play well with others. We can't afford to be the one who put you in touch with a showrunner if you over-talk, get angry when you're given a note, or just plain act up. Just like you, our reputations are on the line. It's rare that you get to make a good first impression twice, and since news travels fast, make sure you have yourself in check before you present yourself to someone you want to start a relationship with.

I've met quite a few people who didn't pass the test. They're easy to spot on email. They're the ones who deliver rambling missives on why they are the most talented person I will ever come across and demand that I take a meeting with them. A few years ago, I received a letter written in crayon. Another fellow sent me a lengthy note and attached twenty-three photos of him standing next to various celebrities. There have been close-talkers and those who won't take no for an answer. And while those are the extreme cases that I can see coming from a mile away, the more subtle tells are people who consistently show up late or always have an excuse for why they can't meet a deadline. I'm not talking about being delayed every now and again. Those things happen. What I mean is, demonstrating the kind of behavior that signals they just aren't ready. Those writers may very well be brilliant, Emmy-caliber future showrunners, but if they can't rise up to do the minimum for me, they will eventually disappoint the person I connect them to.

If any of this sounds like you, don't be discouraged. You can right the ship. Take stock of whether this is really the right time for you to pursue your career. Before you put yourself out there, get organized, get centered, and set clear and attainable goals. The first time you connect with an exec, they are assessing whether or not you are someone into whom they should invest their time. Demonstrate that you are by acting professionally and presenting your very best self.

CHAPTER 5

YOUR GAME PLAN

*I*n your head, you know what you want. You've envisioned it a million times. You know what kind of writer you want to be, what kind of platform you'd most like to work on, and you know the kind of content you want to create. Manifesting that dream into a reality, however, takes planning. You need to come to the party prepared. That plan should include knowing your strengths as a writer, having the material to back that up, and being able to articulate to others what you bring to the table.

PICKING YOUR LANE

When you are starting out, you'll be told to pick a lane. This has nothing to do with your ability to write a variety of ideas, or to force you to give up directing or acting in order to pursue writing. It has everything to do with the fact that when you give an executive a specific vision of who you are and what you want, right away we understand how to help you.

We need clear directives. Every minute of the day, our minds are racing with a million other things. When I'm sitting in a meeting with you, I might be thinking, "I really like this writer. I should introduce this person to _____ (fill in the blank)." If I like you and want to help, my goal is to introduce you to someone who can hire you. But if you've just told me you write everything — hour-long fantasy dramas, half-hour romantic comedies, spy thrillers, and period pieces about the Civil War, I'm now stymied and don't know where to send you. By giving me too many options, chances are good that I won't do anything at all. Like eating at a restaurant with a sprawling menu, having a plethora of choices doesn't make the food any better, but it absolutely slows everything down. I need to be able to do that one thing — to send that one intro email, or place that one call — to set you on the right path. It doesn't mean that you can't also be considered for other things, but first things first.

YOUR STOCKPILE

Before you get out of the gate, you will need two strong samples of your writing which will be your calling cards as you enter the marketplace. They should both be in the same general lane, meaning that if you plan to be a drama writer, you should have two drama scripts in your arsenal. If you consider yourself a comedy writer, then those two scripts should both be comedies. It's fine to have two tonally different scripts that show your range as a writer, so long as they stick to your lane. One script could be more broadcast, the other more cable in tone. If you're writing dramas, a procedural and a more character-driven sample is a good mix. In comedy, perhaps one slightly broader in tone and one more sophisticated. What they are about isn't as critical as it is to demonstrate what kind of material you'd like to write.

If you have zero plans of ever writing period pieces, don't write period pieces, because I guarantee that whatever you put out there will become your brand. One of my HBOAccess writing fellows had two sports-themed scripts coming into the program and pitched another sports-themed idea to write as her third piece. After laying out for her that she would be boxing herself into only writing on sports shows, she decided to write a deliciously hard-edged family drama which became her calling card for a variety of other opportunities.

Whatever scripts you put out there are telling a story about who you are as a writer. In the beginning, you will define yourself primarily in terms of either fitting into the comedy or the drama bucket. Over the course of your career, you may ultimately want to stretch those boundaries, but when you're starting out you must have a strategy that leads you in one direction.

Consider this: you've written a horror feature that has caught the eye of the showrunner of *Blood and Guts,* a dark one-hour series. She asks you to send a second sample, but all you have to send her is a half-hour pilot called *The Prince* about a kindergartener hired as the principal of his preschool. This second script won't sync up with the one that the showrunner originally read. She won't be able to gauge whether you have what it takes to sustain yourself in the horror genre and will pass you over for someone with a stronger portfolio. If you'd had two dark dramas, you could send the other one as your second sample and land the job.

TO SPEC OR NOT TO SPEC

But wait, what about a spec of an existing show? Isn't that a critical piece for every portfolio? Yes and no. There are still a few writing programs that require a sample of an existing show. We call those spec scripts, which stands for something written on speculation. In truth, the term "spec" should encompass anything you write before you are paid for it. However, in TV-speak we use it to mean your version of a show that's already on the air.

What is the point of writing an episode of a show that already exists? Until about a decade ago, this was how showrunners and executives assessed whether you could write in someone else's voice. We assumed that if you were able to capture the sound of the characters, you would probably be a good fit for this show or another one like it.

Eventually specs dropped out of favor and submitting original pilots as samples gained popularity. Part of the reason was that everyone grew tired of reading the same rotation of A-list series (shows generally considered to be top-tier, hit shows guaranteed to return the following fall). Imagine how many *Grey's Anatomy,*[51] *House,*[52] or *The Office*[53] specs that were out there.

The other reason was that it was easier to see how inventive and skilled a writer was if the script was of an original idea. If a writer demonstrated intriguing characters and good storytelling even before nabbing a staff position, the chances were good they would be even better after one.

---

[51] https://www.imdb.com/title/tt0413573/
[52] https://www.imdb.com/title/tt0412142/
[53] https://www.imdb.com/title/tt0386676/

The faulty logic that comes with that thinking is the failure to recognize that writing a pilot is a challenge for even the best writers in town. Nobody knocks it out of the park all of the time. If they did, network schedules would be populated only with hit TV series. It's actually unfair to emerging writers to expect them to craft an attention-getting original pilot when they haven't received any guidance first.

That said, you still may want to include a spec of an existing show in your portfolio. Select a show that's been on for at least one season and has some level of critical acclaim or popularity. Of course, it should be in line with your game plan. Don't pick a supernatural thriller if you don't want to write supernatural thrillers.

WRITING SAMPLE EXCEPTIONS

Having two strong originals and a spec is imperative, but there are always exceptions to every rule. There are times when you can use short stories, blogs, plays, and feature scripts, depending on what kind of job you are going up for. Late night shows like to see sketch packets, jokes, or monologues, but the material must be topical, so you have to write those on request. Sending in last month's packet with old jokes will only hurt your chances. You must have fresh material that speaks to what's happening right now.

A Canadian writer I met with told me that she staffed on a sci-fi series based off a short story she'd written. If you're hilarious on Twitter, you may be able to attract a following that can translate into something more. In short, there are options when it comes to building your body of work. Don't rule anything out.

The problem with only having a few pieces of material is that you will burn through it faster than you think. Your first script is a door opener. It will show folks that you can write and give them a sense of the kind of material you want to work on. You will be surprised, though, how quickly it will circulate around town and people will ask for a second piece of material to confirm that you are sustainable and haven't just been rewriting that same piece for the past seven years.

This is where your second script comes into play. The town will want to confirm that if you're given an assignment, or get on staff, you can deliver. If you only have one sample, we will know for sure you're not all that committed to this line of work.

Having an equally strong third script, or some other piece of material, will keep the doors open. A successful writer friend of mine delivers his reps a new piece of material every few months. It keeps him working because his managers prefer to send out something fresh whenever new opportunities come up.

A MISSION STATEMENT

After spending thirty or so years in the business, I recently made a huge career change by leaping from the development side of the business into the writer ranks with a deal at HBO. I was signed by 3 Arts Entertainment and was on my way. But at the beginning of our relationship, my manager kept sending me very dramatic, historical books. This was my chance to redefine myself in the industry, he counseled. It's a clean slate. Be who you want to be.

The books he sent me were the true stories about fearless figures who had triumphed over terrible circumstances. In the hands of a Barry Jenkins or an Ava Duvernay, these would be amazing and important stories that should be told.

I, on the other hand, considered myself a comedy writer. I look for the funny. Each time I pitched back my take, I could hear my manager's exasperated sighs on the other end of the line. He was sending me gold and I was spinning it into wet, trampled on hay. I just wasn't getting it.

Finally, I called a seasoned showrunner with decades of success under his belt, who wisely suggested that I write a mission statement. Not only would it define for myself what kind of material I wanted to write, it would give me the language I needed to tell my reps and ensure there was no misunderstanding going forward.

This is what I wrote:

Mission Statement: I'm not ashamed to say that I love happy endings. I love movies with humor and wonder. I'm not big on things steeped in pain or suffering. There are many wonderful dramatic writers who can write about sadness and serial killers much, much better than I.

I want to write things where the hair on the back of your neck goes up, you get choked up, you can't turn the pages fast enough because you know what's coming and can't wait until it gets here, or maybe, you don't even see it coming at all. I like surprises and twists and I like to have fun along the way.

Think of me as a 30% bitchier version of Nora Ephron.

Here are things I wish I'd written:

Field of Dreams[54]
A Beautiful Mind[55]
The Long Shot[56]
The Professional[57]
Searching[58]
Role Models[59]
The Sixth Sense[60]
Anything with the name *Jason Bourne*[61] in it
The Karate Kid[62] (because when he does the crane it is absolutely everything)
Good Girls[63]
The Philadelphia Story[64] (except for the part where Grant pushes Hepburn onto the floor)
Pleasantville[65]
The Newsroom[66]

And a list of things that would never, in a zillion years, cross my mind to write:

---

[54] https://www.imdb.com/title/tt0097351/
[55] https://www.imdb.com/title/tt0268978/
[56] https://www.imdb.com/title/tt0385638/
[57] https://www.imdb.com/title/tt0110413/
[58] https://www.imdb.com/title/tt7668870/
[59] https://www.imdb.com/title/tt0430922/
[60] https://www.imdb.com/title/tt0167404/
[61] https://www.imdb.com/title/tt0258463/
[62] https://www.imdb.com/title/tt0087538/
[63] https://www.imdb.com/title/tt6474378/
[64] https://www.imdb.com/title/tt0032904/
[65] https://www.imdb.com/title/tt0120789/
[66] https://www.imdb.com/title/tt0115291/

Goodfellas[67]
Breaking Bad[68]
New Jack City[69]
Call Me By Your Name[70]
The Handmaid's Tale[71]
Scarface[72]

Writing that mission statement helped me zero in on who I wanted to be as a writer and helped my manager focus on what fits best inside my wheelhouse. Sidestepping projects that are better served for other writers frees me up to work on things that excite and energize me.

Figure out who you are and what you want to write. It should be short, succinct, and clear. Write down a few examples of films, series, shorts, or books you wish you'd written and a few that held absolutely no interest for you at all. Try to discern what interests you. Consider the themes that repeatedly pop up. Pay close attention to the feeling in your stomach when you see something that inspires you. Why does it capture your imagination? Put all of that on a piece of paper and see if it sums up who you are as a writer.

Don't worry, you aren't married to it. These are only words on a paper and you can change them at any time. For now, this will help you get laser-focused on your next steps.

---

[67] https://www.imdb.com/title/tt0099685/
[68] https://www.imdb.com/title/tt0903747/
[69] https://www.imdb.com/title/tt0102526/
[70] https://www.imdb.com/title/tt5726616/
[71] https://www.imdb.com/title/tt5834204/
[72] https://www.imdb.com/title/tt0086250/

THE EXTRAS

In addition to your samples, you will also need a bio or resume to send out with your scripts or to apply to industry writing programs. The bio should be short, no longer than half a page, and should outline your career path and your passion for storytelling. Even if you're just graduating from college, you've spent time honing your craft. You've joined theater clubs, worked crew on a short film, taken courses in screenwriting, created a website, or written plays. It's all relevant to how you've reached this point in your career.

If opting for a resume, organize it to tell a story about how much you love the business, and what you've done to push yourself forward. It's not necessary to include every internship if it isn't relevant to entertainment. Be selective.

The last must-have item will be your headshot. Why? Because when you win that contest or get that job, *Deadline*, *Variety*, and the *Hollywood Reporter* will want to put it in your announcement. You'll also need it for panel discussion flyers, alumni association events, and competitions you apply for. It never ceases to amaze me how many writing and directing fellows didn't have a decent photo I could put into the press release. Even if you don't think you'll need it anytime soon, have a friend snap a well-lit profile pic on a generic background and file it away in a desktop folder. You'll thank me later.

WHERE THE ACTION IS

Now that you have a game plan for what you're putting on the page, you'll need to figure out how you go about infiltrating the business. Luckily, the world is transitioning to a mobile economy and, these days, you can work remotely from practically anywhere. Because of this new flexibility, people have become subject matter experts from the comfort of their own homes. This is great news for anyone who doesn't currently live in New York, L.A., or one of the other entertainment hubs. For certain, we've learned that it's possible to be more flexible with our work arrangements. However, there are a few reasons you may still need to be where the action happens.

Reason number one: People like to work with people they know.

Hollywood is a social town, and folks like to work with people they trust or who have been vouched by someone they know. The only way to get that sense of familiarity is in person. When you've met someone face to face, or worked with them day in and day out on staff, you get an idea of how they work in a team setting. You know if they play well in the sandbox and what their strengths and weaknesses are. You can also gauge how they are when you introduce them to others. Think of the people you call on when you're in a bind. They're the ones you know well and can count on, not someone you've met once over a thirty-minute Zoom.

Reason number two: Availability to meet in person

Hollywood meetings are often canceled. Emergencies come up. More important meetings are slotted in place of less important ones. Any number of things can bump something off the schedule. But meetings are the only way for someone to vouch for you so that you can be hired.

Let's say you live in Michigan. You come to Los Angeles once every three or four months to take a few meetings. Whoever is helping you get that meeting is going to have to work miracles to set that get-together within your one-week timeframe. Now they're working on your schedule. And if, for some reason, that meeting gets pushed, it might not happen again for another three to four months, if at all.

It's not uncommon for meetings to be rescheduled multiple times before they actually happen, so being flexible is key. On the other hand, if you're here in Los Angeles, you can be available whenever that important person has an opening.

BEFORE YOU PACK. . .

Before you make the big trek to Hollywood, try establishing a presence from where you are. Let your reputation precede you by using your Twitter and Instagram posts, your website, your blog, or your YouTube channel to get noticed. If you absolutely abhor social media, this won't work for you, because your output has to be consistent. But if posting regularly is in your DNA, building a following online can help pave the way to new and unexpected relationships. When Last Week Tonight was looking for writers, the show asked for topical, comedic journalists.

Not surprisingly, social media became one of our best resources for tapping into these new voices.

Before I stepped away from being an executive and transitioned to writing full time, I posted a series of stories on Facebook about riding the bus in L.A. Giving up a car in favor of public transportation may not seem like a big deal in other cities, but this was absolutely unheard of in L.A. My friends are used to riding solo in their four-wheeled bubbles, and had a hard time understanding why anyone would give up that freedom. I had spent years commuting over an hour to the office and back, white knuckling it on the freeway in slow-moving rush hour traffic. After years of torture, I loathed the idea of getting into my car.

One day, I simply refused to struggle anymore, and started taking the bus. And, from the first time I stepped onto the 734 to Westwood, I felt like I was having a spa day. Not only was I happier and less stressed, I also started engaging with my city in a whole new way. I visited stores I had never noticed before, met interesting and sometimes baffling people, and had conversations I would never have had sitting alone in my car.

Documenting my travels on social media had a surprising side-effect on my career. A friend who had read my posts recommended them to the executive in charge of selecting fellows for the Sundance Episodic Lab. Without even intending to, I had already created a valuable platform for myself as a writer.

Another avenue to consider is applying for programs and competitions which will help you connect to a whole new group of contacts. Many are free to enter. Some are not. Some take place virtually, while others might be located outside of major cities or even overseas. The good news is, there are many more ways to get noticed now than there were ten years ago. As technology improves our ability to find you, your chances of being found increase exponentially. Use whatever you can from wherever you are to shine light on your talent.

CRAFTING YOUR PERSONAL NARRATIVE

Once you get here, you'll need to be able to tell us all about yourself. Your personal story should be compelling, but told in a well-encapsulated five to fifteen minutes. After all, you are not synopsizing *War and Peace*[73]; this is the highlight reel of your life as a creative entity.

The process is something I call Crafting Your Personal Narrative. All you have to do is take a large piece of paper (my favorites are the giant 3M post-it notes that stick to the wall), and with a large Sharpie, draw the six or seven seminal events that have made you the writer you are today. There's only one rule: you cannot write any words on your page. No matter how embarrassing your artistic talents might be, you may only draw pictures. Drawing engages another part of your brain which prevents you from self-editing. Getting to the core of how you became who you are today is what this exercise is all about. Let's get to it.

Start by drawing an oval in the center of the page.

---

[73] https://www.imdb.com/title/tt0049934/

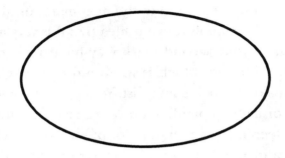

Then add seven tick marks around the outside.

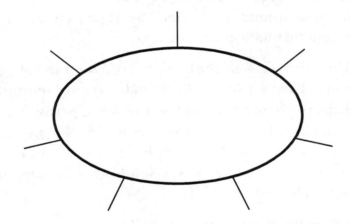

Each mark will represent a significant event in your life that has put you on the path to being a creative. At the first mark on the top left, draw whatever symbol reminds you of your birthplace. When someone says "tell me about yourself" you will probably start with where you were born, so draw whatever picture comes to mind when you think of that location. Make it one thing, not a landscape com-position. We're operating in the land of stick figures, not replicating Monet.

Now, continue around to the next mark, until you finish adding in symbols for your life up to this very moment.
As a guide, your second mark may be around the time
you were thirteen, which is when most people discover
their passion for being an artist. Yours might come a little
sooner or later, depending on your particular life events,
but thirteen is a seminal time for pre-teens. It's when our
bodies and our communities recognize the transition
from childhood to adulthood. It's also when we discover
how we're different from our friends. Our talents have
begun to emerge, and we begin to distinguish ourselves
from those around us in some way. Figure out a way to
represent that time in one drawing.

The third mark might be where you went to college.
You may have started to finally take writing seriously.
Perhaps you wrote a one-act play or saw a performance
that changed how you viewed the world. None of this
is set in stone so feel free to play with a few different
key moments. Whatever it is, it will likely correlate with
young adulthood.

Follow the same pattern around the oval, until all of
the tick marks have pictures next to them, bringing you
up to the present. This last mark should correlate to where
you are now. If you've squeezed in an extra mark, it's too
many. I once had a program participant try to squish in
twenty life events. It meant that she wasn't thinking macro
enough about what impacted her journey to becoming
a writer. These should be life-changing moments where
you felt there was a dividing line — a definite "before"
and "after."

Going through a divorce created that kind of before and after in my own life. In my before, I had followed all of the rules — I married, bought a house, had three kids, and adopted a menagerie of pets. In my after, I decided that all bets were off. I found myself living more fully and more joyfully. I applied to Emerson for my MFA in Writing for Film and Television, and applied to Sundance — two things I never would have done during my marriage.

Choose those big personal revelations significant to your story. They might include a traumatic event, a cross-country move, living abroad, winning a championship, living with an insane family, feeling like an outcast at school, or the time you read that extraordinary book that changed everything. The beautiful thing about these seven marks are they are yours. You craft the story. This is your personal roadmap.

Now we get to the center. That giant empty hole in the middle of your page. Did you think we were just going to leave that blank? This might be the most important part yet. This is your chance to dream.

In the center of the oval, draw a picture of where you want to be in the future. If you want to write on a show, draw a pen, a script, a computer, or a table with people around it for a writer's room. If you also want to direct, you may want to draw a camera. Whatever it is, it should represent how you envision the next step in your career. Don't forget, we're going to keep an open mind for how this might manifest. Don't draw the logo for a specific network or studio, because you might not end up there. Placing limitations on yourself early on closes you off to bigger and better opportunities than what you currently see in front of you. Drawing an idea of what you hope for your future is just like drawing on your vision board.

There is a 100% chance that, at the end of your meeting, someone will ask you "So, what do you see yourself doing?" This mark is the answer to that question. If possible, it should be something actionable. The person doing the asking probably can't help you win an Emmy, but they probably can make a valuable introduction to someone who is hiring for a show.

Now you have a filled-out diagram. This is the outline for the story of your life.

Here's your next step: tell your story to someone.

Make sure you pick an emotionally supportive friend, because what you say will be incredibly personal, and you will need a safe environment on your first go-round. Your friend must agree to keep what you say in the cone of silence. This is soul-baring stuff, and you will be vulnerable. At first, your story will be disorganized, perhaps even coming in fits and starts, and that's perfectly okay. You are in your rough draft stage.

Then, ask your friend to give you feedback. They should be listening for anything in particular that stands out. Ask what they remembered most. What sections did they want to know more about? When did they lean in or start to check out? If there was a moment where your voice caught and became particularly emotional, when was that? Your friend might also hear a pattern in what you are saying. Oftentimes, there's the slightest thread of a theme that runs through our stories that we aren't even aware of ourselves. It might be one of resilience, loss, fighting to belong, or constantly being a fish out of water. Have your friend listen for the theme which will help you with the overall design and shape of your own hero's journey.

After you've heard what pops and what needs a bit more work, like every script you've ever written, you will work on tailoring your thru line until you have a cohesive and coherent narrative.

The thirty-second version of this story will be your "elevator speech." You'll use it when you only have thirty-seconds to introduce yourself to someone in an elevator or at the cocktail party hors d'oeuvres table. For that version, a good template is to say what you do and why you do it. My own elevator speech used to go like this:

"I'm Kelly Edwards. I run the emerging artist programs for HBO and I make people's dreams come true."

Yours doesn't have to be that slogan-y, but this one worked for me because the phrase seemed to stick with people. Everyone has a dream. Wouldn't it be great to make it a reality?

Of the two longer versions of your story, one will be for meetings with executives and the other will be for meetings with showrunners. In many ways, they will be similar, but they will also be slightly different. Your executive meeting will be more top line. You'll still deliver your story, ask them questions about their role at the company, what they're looking for in terms of material, discuss your favorite shows, and connect over people you both know, but this version of your life story will not necessarily plumb the depths of your psyche in the way that you might in a meeting with a showrunner.

Your showrunner meeting will demand another layer of commitment from you. Their goal is to find out if you have a reservoir of stories inside of you, if you're open enough to share them in a room, and if you will play well with others. Showrunners are looking for the right combination of personalities to bring together to aid in the creation of a series. They don't want folks who dominate or derail the conversation. They're also not interested in combative writers who insist on their ideas over anyone else's.

What they do want are people who bring something to the table, are collaborative, and get along with their fellow staff members. In addition, they want writers who will share their personal stories. A friend, who worked on a popular legal drama likened their writer's room to a daily therapy session. Vulnerability was celebrated as writers shared their personal traumas in search of powerful stories to use in the show. While that level of exposure might not be your thing, you should be prepared and willing to mine your life's experiences to some extent.

You are the hero of your own story. Craft it to tell the tale you want to tell. You choose which parts to include and which to leave out, whether you infuse it with a theme, or just list the facts. Depending on the circumstance, you can tell a different version to a whole new audience. Most importantly, you can change it at any time. It's your story.

CHAPTER 6

THE PITCH

You sit in a cavernous office, across from the unblinking eyes of a team of television network executives. Your pulse races, your stomach tightens. Perspiration beads on your forehead and pools in the small recess just above your upper lip. You're about to dazzle them about an idea you have worked on for months. And, after a polite warm up, everyone looks to you to begin your pitch.

It's a terrifying scenario. No wonder so many people find pitching an excruciating process. For even the most experienced writers and producers, pitching is something to be feared and avoided at all costs. And yet, it's the only way for a project to move forward. For someone to buy your idea, you must first pitch it to them.

But pitching isn't just for writers trying to sell a project. Even if you are lucky enough to sell a spec script, you will still have to sit in a room with a group of executives and pitch your vision for the series. While writers do the lion's share of pitching in Hollywood, oftentimes executives have to pitch as well.

These days, it's rare for an exec to have buying power in the room, so an exec often has to run the idea up the flagpole to their boss before being able to make the deal. Our pitch for the show will not be anywhere near as detailed as that of the writer who initially came in to sell it. For the executive, it may be a one-line pitch, or maybe a conversation about why they want to move forward on it, but it's still a pitch. This version of the pitch will only contain a logline or short summary of the show idea, a mention of the writer's credits and the elements attached, coupled with a great deal of enthusiasm to push it over the edge. An exec's pitching skills are critical to building the development slate they want to work on that year.

As a manager in Fox's comedy department, I was expected to bring at least ten new show ideas to our Monday morning staff meetings. I was new at this. I'd come from features, where executives never pitched out ideas on a weekly basis. An agent would send you a script, you'd read it, do coverage, and either send it through with a recommendation, or a pass. But my boss wanted fresh ideas every week.

It was a tall order. I'd never come up with television ideas before. Back then, Fox was mostly airing reality cop shows interspersed with high concept comedies and *The Tracey Ullman Show,*[74] which was about to spawn an animated series based on a series of interstitials called *The Simpsons.*[75] *Beverly Hills 90210*[76] also had a spot on the schedule, as did Kenan Ivory Wayans' *In Living Color.*[77] The wildly inventive *The Ben Stiller Show*[78] had recently been canceled. Martin Lawrence's half-hour sitcom *Martin* was

---

[74] https://www.imdb.com/title/tt0092469/
[75] https://www.imdb.com/title/tt0096697/
[76] https://www.imdb.com/title/tt0098749/
[77] https://www.imdb.com/title/tt0098830/
[78] https://www.imdb.com/title/tt0103360/

just launching, soon to be followed by a show called *Shaky Ground*, [79] starring Matt Frewer of *Max Headroom* [80] fame.

While CBS, NBC, and ABC had strong identities, Fox was still searching for its brand. CBS and ABC were known for their family shows. It was easy for a writer to look at their schedules and know what to pitch them. CBS had strong female leads in their lineup, like *Designing Women* and *Murphy Brown*. ABC's TGIF (Thank God It's Friday) lineup was family-friendly sitcoms like *Step by Step* [81] and *Family Matters*. [82] NBC was building its Must See TV lineup with "sophisticated urban comedies" like *Cheers, Wings, Mad About You*, [83] and *Seinfeld*. [84] Fox's schedule of off-beat shows had yet to coalesce into an easily understandable tagline. The typical response we'd get when asking an agent to meet with their writer was, "I'll tell my client you want to meet, but what exactly is a Fox show?"

Eventually, the answer became "anything you wouldn't see on the other networks." Edgy fare. Ideas that pushed the limits, were topical, or, as we liked to say, "taboo." But for writers and the agents pitching those writers, knowing what that meant was something else altogether.

This meant that as Fox continued to build its lineup, it was on us to pitch out ideas to bring writers into the tent. No writer wanted to spend time spinning their wheels to maybe come up with something Fox might buy. We needed to be specific and tell them exactly what we were looking for.

---

[79] https://www.imdb.com/title/tt0103541/
[80] https://www.imdb.com/title/tt0092402/
[81] https://www.imdb.com/title/tt0101205/
[82] https://www.imdb.com/title/tt0096579/
[83] https://www.imdb.com/title/tt0103484/
[84] https://www.imdb.com/title/tt0098904/

On Monday mornings, we'd come to our staff meeting to pitch areas and ideas, many of which ended up as pilots or shows on our air. If one of our pitches got the stamp of approval, we'd pick a writer to pitch it to and see if they had a "take" on the idea.

My boss, however, was not an easy audience. Coming up with a concept that met his approval proved to be a tough sell, and early on, I often failed to impress him. I knew that if I were to succeed, I needed to get much better at pitching out the thoughts in my head. And so, I practiced. I organized my ideas in a clear structure, used my voice to give a sense of tone, and then told the story. Little did I know that learning how to pitch effectively would be a skill I would use throughout my career.

As I rose through the ranks to SVP, I found myself pitching ideas both externally to writers I was courting to work at the network, and internally to my bosses to sell the ideas I wanted them to buy. When we set our schedules in May, I was back at it again. By then our pilots had been screened for senior management and each exec would have rated his or her picks based on everything that had been produced that season. Some of the shows were targeted for immediate placement on the schedule, but a few others would be held for a mid-season launch.

The team stood in a conference room in front of a large, colorful chart with magnetic tiles labeled with show titles. We'd look at a mock-up of what we guessed was going to be our competition's schedule, and build a case for what we thought would make the strongest programming to win the night. Pitching the shows I wanted to green light was nerve-racking. I was emotionally invested in all of them. These pitches counted.

Not every show I championed made the schedule. One particularly painful loss didn't even make it to pilot. I was running comedy for UPN, and had received a script called *Malcolm in the Middle* from Rick Rosen, at Endeavor. Right away, I knew it was perfect for UPN. We had been searching for a brand and this was it — an outrageous family comedy loosely based on Linwood Boomer's life about a smart pre-teen relentlessly tortured by his oddball brothers and raised by two unconventional parents.

I pitched hard for *Malcolm.* But at the time, the network president wanted UPN to program family-friendly comedies like ABC, and *Malcolm* wasn't in line with his vision. In the end, we passed on the project. It was particularly heartbreaking when my good friend, who was running comedy at Fox at the time, called me to say she had bought the script and was going straight to pilot.

"Thanks for a perfect script," she said, "No notes."

KNOW WHAT WE BUY AND WHAT WE'VE BOUGHT

One of the worst things to hear after delivering a good pitch is "Thanks, but we already have something just like it in development." It's a surefire kiss of death, but it's completely avoidable if you've done your homework and know what a network has already bought.

Sometimes a producer might call the network in advance and "float the idea" by them. They may say they've got a family show set in the world of finance, or be even more specific and run the logline by the network. Whatever the big idea of the pitch you are taking in, hopefully you've pre-sold it before you get in the room.

Before you can even set foot inside a development executive's office, however, you have to understand the network's brand. You must be well versed in what the network currently has on the air, the types of shows they tend to buy, what their schedule is lacking, what producers they like to work with, and a whole host of other information that you should already know because you're a fan. Your producer, studio, and reps will also be able to help you with this, since part of their job is to stay on top of what's happening competitively between the networks.

Bone up on the profile of the company you are pitching. Avoid taking your slasher idea to Disney+ and your sad family drama to Comedy Central. It helps to know that CBS and NBC lean heavily into procedural dramas. CBS shows are considered more meat and potatoes series, appealing to an older crowd. Their crime show franchises stick to a distinct formula, while NBC might venture into high concept hours and reliable staples like Dick Wolf 's *Chicago* and *Law and Order* series. Figure out if a network wants more of the same, or whether they are angling to switch things up a bit. It will help you when you try to sell them your show. Having the inside track on the network's plans can save you from going in with the wrong idea at the wrong time.

KNOW WHO WE LIKE

Every network has an unofficial list of actors and writers they would love to work with. There are also unofficial lists of actors and writers they would never work with. Knowing who a network likes and doesn't like could mean the difference between whether they buy your project or they pass politely. Why is this important? Because you may find you want to make your project more interesting by attaching a piece of talent or a showrunner to your idea. If your reps, production company, or studio thinks that getting a heavy hitter to come aboard your project could help sell it, you might want to add that element before you go in to the network. Studios sometimes have overall deals with big-name executive producers who are looking to shepherd a younger writer. The agency or management company that reps you might have an actor that means something in the marketplace and may want to attach that talent to create a sexier package.

However, not all networks like all of the same names. They may have had bad experiences with a particular showrunner. They might not think that the actor can carry a show on their own. You also might decide not to attach talent at all. Instead, you might decide to mention a few names of potential actors in the room. Do the research. Ask around. Not all names carry the same weight, and some may actually hurt your chances should you bring up the wrong one.

KNOW OUR REFERENCES

I Love Lucy,[85] *The Mary Tyler Moore Show,*[86] *Homicide: Life on the Street,*[87] *Frasier, Breaking Bad, Mad Men,*[88] *The Sopranos, The Walking Dead,*[89] *Friends,*[90] and *The Shield.*[91] What do all of these shows have in common?

Absolutely nothing, other than that they are frequently referenced in meetings with executives. Whether iconic, groundbreaking, or just wildly popular, these shows become our way of short handing ideas. Mary Tyler Moore is the quintessential single working woman. When someone references Lucy, it usually has to do with her physical comedy. If you're at all unfamiliar with anything on the list below, now's the perfect time for you to dig in and get acquainted with some of the best our business has to offer.

Naturally, the list grows with each passing season, as new series update our reference points. It will be up to you to keep pace with what's currently considered water-cooler content. And don't stop with just TV. Include films, podcasts, and web series in your education.

This list is by no means exhaustive. It's simply to get you started on a never-ending journey into discovering brilliant content. Enjoy.

---

[85] https://www.imdb.com/title/tt0043208/
[86] https://www.imdb.com/title/tt0065314/
[87] https://www.imdb.com/title/tt0106028/
[88] https://www.imdb.com/title/tt0804503/
[89] https://www.imdb.com/title/tt1520211/
[90] https://www.imdb.com/title/tt0108778/
[91] https://www.imdb.com/title/tt0286486/

Series:

All in the Family[92]

Ally McBeal[93]

American Horror Story

Big Little Lies[94]

Buffy the Vampire Slayer[95]

CSI: Crime Scene Investigation[96]

Cheers

Dawson's Creek[97]

ER[98]

Frasier

Friends

Girlfriends

Green Acres[99]

Grey's Anatomy

Homicide: Life on the Streets

How I Met Your Mother[100]

How to Get Away with Murder[101]

I Love Lucy

In Living Color

Julia[102]

Living Single

Mad Men

Martin

M.A.S.H.[103]

NCIS

[92] https://www.imdb.com/title/tt0066626/
[93] https://www.imdb.com/title/tt0118254/
[94] https://www.imdb.com/title/tt3920596/
[95] https://www.imdb.com/title/tt0118276/
[96] https://www.imdb.com/title/tt0247082/
[97] https://www.imdb.com/title/tt0118300/
[98] https://www.imdb.com/title/tt0108757/
[99] https://www.imdb.com/title/tt0058808/
[100] https://www.imdb.com/title/tt0460649/
[101] https://www.imdb.com/title/tt3205802/
[102] https://www.imdb.com/title/tt0062575/
[103] https://www.imdb.com/title/tt0068098/

NYPD Blue[104]

Orange Is the New Black[105]

Sanford and Son[106]

Saturday Night Live[107]

Scandal[108]

Seinfeld

Star Trek[109]

Succession[110]

The Adventures of Ozzie and Harriet[111]

The Andy Griffith Show[112]

The Big Bang Theory[113]

The Brady Bunch[114]

The Crown[115]

The Golden Girls

The Handmaid's Tale

The Jeffersons[116]

The Mary Tyler Moore Show

The Practice[117]

The Queen's Gambit[118]

The Sopranos

The Twilight Zone[119]

The Wire[120]

Ugly Betty[121]

[104] https://www.imdb.com/title/tt0106079/
[105] https://www.imdb.com/title/tt2372162/
[106] https://www.imdb.com/title/tt0068128/
[107] https://www.imdb.com/title/tt0072562/
[108] https://www.imdb.com/title/tt1837576/
[109] https://www.imdb.com/title/tt0060028/
[110] https://www.imdb.com/title/tt7660850/
[111] https://www.imdb.com/title/tt0044230/
[112] https://www.imdb.com/title/tt0053479/
[113] https://www.imdb.com/title/tt0898266/
[114] https://www.imdb.com/title/tt0063878/
[115] https://www.imdb.com/title/tt4786824
[116] https://www.imdb.com/title/tt0072519/
[117] https://www.imdb.com/title/tt0118437/
[118] https://www.imdb.com/title/tt10048342
[119] https://www.imdb.com/title/tt0052520/
[120] https://www.imdb.com/title/tt0306414/
[121] https://www.imdb.com/title/tt0805669/

Films:

12 Years A Slave[122]
2001: A Space Odyssey[123]
A Clockwork Orange[124]
Alien[125]
Apocalypse Now[126]
Blade Runner[127]
Boyz n the Hood[128]
Casablanca[129]
Citizen Kane[130]
Close Encounters of the Third Kind[131]
Coming to America[132]
Do the Right Thing[133]
Easy Rider[134]
Ferris Bueller's Day Off[135]
Fight Club[136]
Friday[137]
Ghostbusters
Goodfellas
Guess Who's Coming to Dinner[138]
Heaven's Gate[139]
Hustle & Flow[140]

[122] https://www.imdb.com/title/tt2024544/
[123] https://www.imdb.com/title/tt0062622/
[124] https://www.imdb.com/title/tt0066921/
[125] https://www.imdb.com/title/tt0078748/
[126] https://www.imdb.com/title/tt0078788/
[127] https://www.imdb.com/title/tt0083658/
[128] https://www.imdb.com/title/tt0101507/
[129] https://www.imdb.com/title/tt0034583/
[130] https://www.imdb.com/title/tt0033467/
[131] https://www.imdb.com/title/tt0075860/
[132] https://www.imdb.com/title/tt0094898/
[133] https://www.imdb.com/title/tt0097216/
[134] https://www.imdb.com/title/tt0064276/
[135] https://www.imdb.com/title/tt0091042/
[136] https://www.imdb.com/title/tt0137523/
[137] https://www.imdb.com/title/tt0113118/
[138] https://www.imdb.com/title/tt0061735/
[139] https://www.imdb.com/title/tt0080855/
[140] https://www.imdb.com/title/tt0410097/

It's a Wonderful Life [141]

Jaws [142]

Love Jones [143]

Midnight Cowboy [144]

Monty Python and the Holy Grail [145]

North by Northwest [146]

One Flew Over the Cuckoo's Nest [147]

Poetic Justice [148]

Precious [149]

Psycho [150]

Pulp Fiction [151]

Raging Bull [152]

Raiders of the Lost Ark [153]

Rocky [154]

Scarface [155]

Selma [156]

Set It Off [157]

Star Wars [158]

Taxi Driver [159]

The Best Man [160]

The Birds [161]

---

[141] https://www.imdb.com/title/tt0038650/
[142] https://www.imdb.com/title/tt0073195/
[143] https://www.imdb.com/title/tt0119572/
[144] https://www.imdb.com/title/tt0064665/
[145] https://www.imdb.com/title/tt0071853/
[146] https://www.imdb.com/title/tt0053125/
[147] https://www.imdb.com/title/tt0073486/
[148] https://www.imdb.com/title/tt0107840/
[149] https://www.imdb.com/title/tt0929632/
[150] https://www.imdb.com/title/tt0054215/
[151] https://www.imdb.com/title/tt0110912/
[152] https://www.imdb.com/title/tt0081398/
[153] https://www.imdb.com/title/tt0082971/
[154] https://www.imdb.com/title/tt0075148/
[155] https://www.imdb.com/title/tt0086250/
[156] https://www.imdb.com/title/tt1020072/
[157] https://www.imdb.com/title/tt0117603/
[158] https://www.imdb.com/star-wars/
[159] https://www.imdb.com/title/tt0075314/
[160] https://www.imdb.com/title/tt0168501/
[161] https://www.imdb.com/title/tt0056869/

The Godfather[162]
The Graduate[163]
The Matrix
The Princess Bride[164]
The Shawshank Redemption[165]
The Usual Suspects[166]
Tootsie[167]
Toy Story[168]

Podcasts:

1619[169]
Crime Junkie[170]
Homecoming[171]
Lore[172]
Pod Save America[173]
Pod Save The People[174]
Scriptnotes[175]
Serial[176]
This American Life[177]

---

[162] https://www.imdb.com/title/tt0068646/
[163] https://www.imdb.com/title/tt0061722/
[164] https://www.imdb.com/title/tt0093779/
[165] https://www.imdb.com/title/tt0111161/
[166] https://www.imdb.com/title/tt0114814/
[167] https://www.imdb.com/title/tt0084805/
[168] https://www.imdb.com/title/tt0114709/
[169] https://www.nytimes.com/column/1619-project
[170] https://crimejunkiepodcast.com/
[171] https://gimletmedia.com/shows/homecoming
[172] https://www.lorepodcast.com/
[173] https://crooked.com/podcast-series/pod-save-america/
[174] https://crooked.com/podcast-series/pod-save-the-people/
[175] https://johnaugust.com/scriptnotes
[176] https://serialpodcast.org/
[177] http://feed.thisamericanlife.org/talpodcast

IDEAS ARE A DIME A DOZEN, IT'S ALL ABOUT EXECUTION

Every now and again, you will hear that someone has sued a company for stealing their idea. And every now and again, there will be some kernel of validity to that claim. But more often than not, it's just a matter of an idea being in the zeitgeist of a particular time in our culture.

Around 2000, there was a massive movement out of the big city toward more rural living. People were leaving the rat race in favor of a simpler lifestyle. They were quitting their high-stress jobs as Wall Street traders and moving to small towns to take up crafting, scrapbooking, and collecting twigs in the woods to fashion into Martha Stewart-like centerpieces. Not surprisingly, pitch after pitch came in about successful, but unhappy, urbanites chucking it all away to move to rough it like the locals.

Every writer who brought that pitch was absolutely certain theirs was the only one. They were on the cutting edge of a new trend. But they were wrong.

Ideas come and go. They come in waves because we're all basically feeling the same way, reading the same magazines, and seeing the same news reports. And that is why television executives aren't so much interested in what you are writing as they are on how you are writing it. You might come in with a similar pitch as the best writer in town. Your pitch might even be better. But if the best writer in town wants to do it, we're going to bet on the fastest horse with the better pedigree. The reason for that is, that once the development process begins, things change and as it moves closer to getting on the air, it might look slightly different from the original pitch.

Even more important than the idea itself is your ability to convey those ideas on paper. When we buy your project, we are buying your expertise. We may not even buy the idea you are currently pitching, but if we love your writing and we like working with you, we will invite you to come back and pitch something else or, better yet, we might even pitch you an idea.

BEING ENGAGING DOES NOT MEAN BEING THEATRICAL

I've only been in one meeting in which theatricality worked. My producing partner, Jonathan Axelrod, and I were working with Gary Scott Thompson, who wrote *The Fast and the Furious,* [178] which, at the time, was just starting its run as one of the most successful feature film franchises in the world. Gary was a big guy with a presence that immediately signaled he was absolutely certain of his craft and his salesmanship.

We were pitching an hour drama to the SVP of Drama Development, Kathy Lingg and her VP of Drama Development Andy Horne, when, during Gary's opening, he slowly rose out of his seat, acting out the final moments of the teaser. Stretching his arms out wide as if holding two handguns, he pointed them at the imaginary assailants and uttered some brilliant phrase that had my heart beating with excitement. Watching that moment unfold

---

[178] https://www.imdb.com/title/tt0232500/

was absolutely exhilarating. I have never seen it work in a pitch again.

In a room of people who have basically seen and heard it all before, there's a 99% chance that acting out your pitch will fall flat. While banter between writing partners sometimes works well, including a gimmicky component in a pitch often doesn't. Sticking to the heart of the show, knowing the characters, and the episode and series arcs is all that is truly needed to sell the concept.

SMALL TALK & THE WIND UP

Every pitch is preceded by two things: small talk and something called the wind up. Small talk is the polite chatter that happens as you enter the executive's office for your pitch. It's designed to warm up the room and make everyone comfortable. It's a chance for you to connect with the executive and for them to get to know you before you tell them your idea.

The small talk can be about anything — the weather, what's going on in the news, what's happening in the industry, sports, personal anecdotes. One particular HBO executive who oversaw *Eastbound and Down*[179] and *Vice Principals*[180] was known around town as a huge sports enthusiast. He kept his office full of football memorabilia which always, and thankfully, sparked conversation and helped break the ice.

Many execs have coffee table books, posters of their successful shows, or photos of their families that can get

---

[179] https://www.imdb.com/title/tt0866442/
[180] https://www.imdb.com/title/tt3766376/

things going. Whatever the conversation starter might be, use it to set a friendly tone. Getting off on the right foot is mission-critical to a smooth beginning.

Immediately following the small talk is the wind up, which is the ramping up that happens before the pitch actually starts. Typically done by your rep, your studio exec, or a combination of you and your partner if you are pitching as a team, someone has to introduce you and give an overview of why this meeting is happening in the first place. The person doing the wind up will give the network a general summary of your background and why you are the perfect person to write the show they are about to hear. A good wind up includes information about how the project came together, who else is involved, and conveys enthusiasm and energy about both you and your concept.

WHY NOW?

Most pitches begin with an overview that answers the question "why now"? Why is your idea relevant at this particular moment in time? When your idea aligns with an urgent need to be told, you have a much better shot of getting it sold.

Not long ago, someone sent me a script they considered a new take on the Western genre, but after reading it, I could see it wasn't really a new take at all. In fact, it played into conventional stereotypes of Black and Indigenous characters that any exec would have had a difficult time justifying as necessary. There was no reason at all to tell that story at this moment and in this way.

The Handmaid's Tale speaks to larger societal issues involving women's rights, while *Speechless*[181] brought the disabled community to the forefront, after largely being absent from the TV landscape. The "why now" could be that it's high time to refresh a forgotten genre or that you have a new spin on an old idea. When you begin with the "why now," you set the table for why we need this show on the air. Impressing us with the themes you are writing about will resonate with us on a deeper level. It gives your pitch urgency and will make us excited to hear more.

WHY YOU?

Whoever's listening to your pitch will want to know why you are the best person to write it. In success, they will be forking over a nice-sized check for you to take on the task of bringing this idea to life. They want to be assured that you are passionate about the subject and that you have a handle on the concept. Tell them why you are the only one who should be entrusted with this idea.

You might have lived the experience or something like it. You might be obsessed with the book, graphic novel, or game since you were sixteen. Maybe you studied the subject in college. How you connect with the area may very well be why you sell this show, so figure out why you were drawn to it and work it into your pitch.

Don't forget, there may be times when the story is not yours to tell. Even though you are fascinated by a particular aspect of a particular ethnic group or race and you are not of that community, you may have to step away from

---

[181] https://www.imdb.com/title/tt5592146/

the idea or partner with someone who has an authentic connection to the material. In this day and age, it's important for writers to be sensitive to who is telling the story. If it's not your experience, leave it to someone else.

THE 30,000-FOOT VIEW

After you give us the "why now" and "why you" of your show, give us the big picture, the 30,000-foot view so we'll have the lay of the land. We need to understand the world we are entering into. Pitching is storytelling. And for us to understand what we're listening to, we have to all be on the same page.

Imagine hearing a story in which you are totally lost. You have no idea why it's being told to you, and you aren't oriented to the where and when. It's impossible to enjoy that story because, in your head, you're spending the majority of your time just trying to figure out who is who and what is what.

Bring us into the world you are exploring by relating it to what's happening in the world right now. Does your idea center on a trend that's being discussed in the papers? Has science made a breakthrough that makes your genre pitch incredibly relevant right now? It might be as simple as giving us insight into how a particular business works before you launch into the characters working that environment. Explaining a dysfunctional family dynamic and how it affects relationships might help us get our footing before you talk about your family drama. Describing a medical condition before diving into the character that suffers from it gives us context before we get to the content.

In order to avoid any confusion, you must give us enough information to let us enjoy what comes next. Starting with the 30,000-foot view and then working your way into the pitch will make sure we're on board.

GRAB OUR ATTENTION

Once the overview is done, you might launch into the opening scene. In a crime drama, this is typically called a "body dump," where the mystery is set up and the ticking clock begins for the hero to track down the killer.

In a medical show, it's the moment where a patient presents with an unusual health issue. In a comedy, this is the teaser that sets up the main character's point of view and gives us a sense of what the situation in the situation comedy will be. Hooking an exec early is the only way to keep their attention. Remember, unless you're the first pitch of the day, the execs you are meeting have already heard a slew of pitches before you entered the room. Tell us a story that grabs us and has us eager to hear more.

KEEP IT TO TWENTY MINUTES

A tight pitch should only be around twenty minutes. Tops. That goes for both comedy and drama. No matter how long your script is on the page, in pitch form twenty minutes is all you'll have before your audience starts to mentally check out. The last thing you want is for someone to start making their grocery list in their head just as you are getting to the good part.

Your twenty minutes does not start during the small talk or the wind up. So, don't feel the need to rush that part of the getting to know you phase. It's only when the spotlight is on you to tell them your idea that the clock begins.

Twenty minutes is all the time you'll need to open with the 30,000-foot view, talk through the opening scene, describe the characters, breeze through the pilot story, and give an overview of the season and series arcs. While you are speaking, the network is listening for clues about how your idea works for them. Is there enough here for a show? Is your character intriguing? How does that hero work with the ensemble you have formed to support him/her?

A good way to practice honing your skills is pitching the pilot for a show that is already on the air. How would you construct it? How would you distill it down to the most pertinent information that still conveys the promise of what it will be when finally produced?

TRY PITCHING IN REVERSE

Trying to pitch a show that is already on the air, where you can see the theme clearly and have some familiarity with the characters, might be a great learning tool in crafting your own pitch. Let's look at *The Handmaid's Tale,* for example.

I wasn't in the room when *The Handmaid's Tale* was pitched to Hulu. However, as an exercise for my writing fellows, I pretended I had been tasked with pitching the opening scene, the characters, the theme, the tone, and the series arc. The pilot is beautifully constructed, so retelling that story as a pitch can be an instructional exercise. From start to finish, the whole thing took about twenty minutes. If *The Handmaid's Tale,* with all of its characters and world-building, is pitch-able in that amount of time, your show can be, too.

My 30,000-foot view opening went something like this:

More than ever, we are seeing the erosion of women's rights happening in real-time. Planned Parenthood is under attack, and *Roe v. Wade* is in imminent danger of being overturned. It all seems to have snuck up on us; however, one writer saw this coming decades ago. That writer was Margaret Atwood, who in 1985 published a novel called *The Handmaid's Tale.* [182]

Why you:

This was one of my favorite books growing up. It's about a world where all women's rights have been stripped away, and women are forced to live under the strict rule of men. Even your body is no longer your own. This dystopian view of society filled me with fear and dread. But what Margaret Atwood imagined as the future has now become our present.

Introduce the format and logline:

The Handmaid's Tale is an hour-long drama series that follows one woman's fight to free herself from a dystopian society that enslaves women and forces them to bear children for barren couples.

---

[182] https://www.britannica.com/topic/The-Handmaids-Tale-by-Atwood

The opening:

We come in overhead as a car careens down a deserted road in the back woods in the middle of nowhere. The sky is gray, as if on the verge of weeping. Inside the car, a man drives as if his life depended on it, his hands on the wheel as he glances back to see if he's being followed. This man is not used to being the hero, he's the guy at the bar who buys the last round. He might even be your brother.

In the backseat, his wife and child cower. Unexceptional, this mom might work in customer service at a Walmart. The child's eyes are shut tight. The mother comforts her. She draws her daughter close, but there is fear in her eyes.

BAM. The car swerves off the road into the woods. The family scrambles out of the car. Knowing they can't all make it, the husband barks at his wife and daughter to go, he'll buy them some time. The woman resists, but she knows he's right. She sees the panic on her daughter's face. Takes her hand. And runs.

They tumble down a hill and hide in the brush. When the mother and child think they're safe, they start again, only to be grabbed by men in black, weapons drawn. Behind them, back where her husband stood his ground, a gunshot rings out through the trees. The mom struggles to hold onto her daughter, but it's no use. A gun cracks into her skull and the one thing she loves more than anything in the world is ripped from her arms.

We cut to a stately brownstone house in what was once an upscale neighborhood. Now this mansion is no more than a beautiful prison. The woman, Offred, thirty, wears a red nun's habit, a white cap covering her face as she looks at the ground. Offred is a Handmaid and today is ceremony day. Commander Waterford is about to impregnate her so that she can bear his wife's child.

Here's how I might end it:

This show is about oppression and slavery and it shows us what happens "when good people do nothing." It's about the rolling back of women's rights. But it's also about the resilience of the human spirit. Because as June (Offred's real name) fights to reclaim her daughter, she will also reclaim herself. She will join the revolution and push herself beyond what she thought were her limited abilities because there is nothing that a mother will not do for her child. Ultimately, every step June takes toward saving her child becomes another step toward saving the world.

Pitched in person, that entire opening would take around four minutes, leaving plenty of time to get into the world and its rules and rituals, the unique language, the plague of infertility, June/Offred's backstory, the supporting characters, and future storylines.

Pick a show that's a comp (comparable) for yours and pitch it backward to yourself or a friend. See if there are elements you can incorporate into your pitch in terms of format, tone, character work, or dramatic effect. You might also want to bring in visuals to help sell the concept. At the very least, it can help you shore up the holes, and at best, may deliver valuable insights into how to make yours a little stronger.

PITCH DECKS, VISUAL AIDS, AND PROOF OF CONCEPTS

In some cases, you may want to bring some kind of visual aid or a leave-behind to help sell your idea. This is completely up to you, and a function of whether or not it will be a value add to your pitch. Years ago, we always cautioned against it because if we loved it in the room, having a document, script, or deck would only serve to unravel the sale, never push it over the edge. Now, pitch decks are more common, though not required.

Include whatever you think will help get your concept across, however, be mindful of the layout and be sure to make it reader friendly. If your eyes gloss over at the amount of text packed onto the page, ours will, too. Keep our attention with just enough information to support the pitch, not to steal focus away from what you're saying.

Mostly used by directors trying to book a pilot, decks convey mood, tone, characters, casting ideas, and overall concept. You can also include series episode ideas and arcs but keep the details light. Don't include too much information in the document. It will overwhelm your audience and leave you nothing to say in the meeting.

Directors also include their visual approach to the material — extreme close ups, subjective point of view, locations — anything to give us insight into their visual style, so if you need to explain how this show is visually unlike anything else we've seen, bringing a deck is a great idea.

Visual aids can also be helpful if your concept is particularly complex. I once took a writer in to pitch a comedy about a sprawling family with a patriarch à la Mick Jagger/ Rod Stewart/Eddie Murphy at the center. With so many ex-wives, girlfriends, and adult children, keeping track of who belonged to whom would have had the network execs struggling to keep up. The deck also allowed us to include the family trees of a number of celebs to show that it was a common phenomenon that could be a great source of comedy.

Shooting a proof of concept can be a terrific way to share your vision of your series, but they can also work against you. Hearing that *Dear White People*[183] started as a proof of concept, was made into a movie, and then went on to success as a TV series can be very enticing. But if your production value isn't what you'd hoped for, or your cast not quite right, you run the risk of sharing work that falls short of what an exec would consider impressive. Justin Simien had an advantage not many of us had. He was working in the marketing department of a major film studio when he shot his attention-getting proof of concept.

Sizzle reels abound on the reality side of the business, but they're still fairly rare in scripted. However, with more festivals holding pilot competitions, it's possible to shoot a short presentation and then use it as a tool to pitch your series. Sundance, ATX, Seriesfest, SXSW, Tribeca, Catalyst, and a host of other festivals offer the opportunity to showcase your work and generate buzz around your idea. You don't even need to win an award. Simply being

---

[183] https://www.imdb.com/title/tt5707802/

chosen to screen at a high-profile fest can be enough to create an amazing halo effect around your project to get you noticed.

EXECUTIVE BODY LANGUAGE

It takes a tremendous amount of effort to develop even the worst pitch. So many variables go into the preparation. You have to make sure the characters are well developed, the story tracks, and there is enough information given to indicate where the series will go. There must be a good balance between giving the network enough to whet their appetite without overselling them.

Ninety percent of pitching is preparation. Only ten percent is the pitch itself; however, that ten percent often makes or breaks the sale. To those doing the selling, getting a yes can mean the difference between paying the mortgage or getting another year's worth of health insurance. Disappointingly, the network's decision whether to move forward or to pass sometimes winds up in the hands of an executive who won't even be at the company in another year. Therefore, the stakes for those sitting on the couch (the pitching side) are incredibly high.

Besides telling a story, your job is to also "read the room." The better pitchers can gauge whether an executive is intrigued by how your concept is unfolding. There are little tells that will show you they're listening. They lean in. Make eye contact. Nod. They ask questions. If you're not getting any verbal or non-verbal cues that they are paying attention, you might want to change things up.

You might stop. Ask if they are following or need clarification. Pause dramatically. Modulate your tone. Go from regular voice to a whisper. Whatever you can do to bring them back to you will help. If things are truly going poorly, you can always stop and ask how you're doing. They may just think the idea isn't right for them. Believe me, they will know early on in your pitch if they're going to buy it or not. Torturing you and themselves is not in either of your best interests. Being able to read the room might help you save the situation and get them to pitch you an area they are looking for. On the other hand, if this is a courtesy meeting and they have no intention of working with you, they won't engage in a discussion about future concepts.

I happened to be in a meeting with my comedy team just after they'd had a pitch that didn't go well. The conversation turned to each executive's "tell" when they'd checked out. It was obvious to everyone that each exec had their own way of signaling to the others that they weren't interested. One tapped his pen, another leaned back in his chair, one doodled on her pad. There are stories about network bigwigs keeping televisions on in the background while people pitched to them. I've even witnessed an exec fall asleep in the middle of a pitch. A drama exec at one of the broadcast nets once famously yelled at a writer to please stop pitching because he was boring her. That kind of response to someone who has spent time and energy on an idea is both unacceptable and, thankfully, rare. The only takeaway from such bad behavior is for you to remain aware of how your pitch is connecting with your audience.

Don't let a cold room deter you. It could have nothing to do with you. It might just be the executive's style. One particular network comedy department was notorious for never laughing at pitches. For many writers, pitching there was a painful experience, since getting no reaction can throw some writers off their game. But that kind of stony silence isn't the norm. For the most part, execs want you to do well. We want to be told a gripping story we haven't heard before, in the intriguing way that only you can tell it. Turn that cold room into a warm one, read our body language, and if we actively stop listening to you, redirect.

DON'T TURN A YES INTO A NO

One consequence of not being able to read the room is that you can ultimately turn a yes into a no. Let's say your pitch has gone well, and the network has bought the idea in the room. The most important thing to do now is not overstay your welcome.

Writers have been known to over-pitch, turning an enthusiastic "we want this" into an "I'm not sure I can work with this writer if they are not self-aware." Remember, the execs want to like working with you. Yes, they are buying your script, but they also know that if this project goes forward, the team will be spending a lot of time with you. But if you don't know when enough is enough, you will find them losing interest not only in your project but also in you.

Get out while the getting's good.

ALWAYS HAVE SOMETHING TO PITCH

The final and most important element of good pitching is having something to pitch in the first place. When writers tell me they don't have anything, I know they're either failing to look inward or failing to look outward.

Each tick mark of your personal story is a potential source of a new pitch. This is your look inward. Take the core of that experience and turn it on its head, set it in a new location, or simply drill down into it as it is. At the center of it is a relationship dynamic you can use as a springboard. We tend to think of our own stories as not particularly interesting. If we haven't had a major tragedy or overcome a terrible situation, we can't possibly be the source of story. And yet, if we look just a little deeper under our own hood, we find plenty of drama and comedy with which to work.

In looking outward, start with the obvious — read books, watch the news, Google random facts, search for public domain titles. Take those things you're drawn to and combine them with something totally random. Case in point, *Cowboys & Aliens*[184] with Daniel Craig. Yes, it's a movie, but somebody thought that up and attached James Bond to star in it.

I like to prompt my fellows to do a fast magazine drill. I toss a stack of random mags covering a variety of interests onto the conference table and give them twenty minutes to come up with show ideas by ripping out the pages of anything they find even remotely interesting. Think you can't find a cool idea by reading about bass fishing,

[184] https://www.imdb.com/title/tt0409847/

motocross, or survivalist prepping? Think again. When the twenty minutes are up, they'd have to pitch the rest of the group their ideas in logline form, with a character, goal, and obstacle. The writers never failed to come up with something unique and fresh. At this point, you don't need a fully fleshed out idea. The goal is to float an "area you're working on."

With a little preparation, an unwavering enthusiasm for your project, and a few deep breaths, pitching does get better, especially when you get a call on Monday morning from an exec who tells you "we love your show and want to buy it."

CHAPTER 7

THE PILOT SCRIPT

*E*very exec wants to find the next *Sopranos*. We want to take credit for discovering a new Diablo Cody. As we reach for your script, more than anything, we're hoping it will be great. That it will be a page-turner so engrossing we won't be able to put it down.

What is the secret formula to getting noticed?

Unfortunately, there isn't one. There is no magic wand to wave over your laptop, no pixie dust to sprinkle onto the pages. Writing is a process that requires passion, time, energy, and a tiny bit of insanity. After all, who in their right mind would want to torture themselves in this kind of way?

The silver lining is that, while there is no trick to writing an amazing pilot, there are a few things you can do to punch through the clutter and stay on our radar.

THE BEST IDEAS ARE PERSONAL

Time and again, I've seen the same thing play out. A writer comes up with a cool concept with lots of bells and whistles. It's clever and twisty, quirky and funny. But by the time we're done reading the first ten pages, we set it aside and click open the next script in the queue.

Why? Because what we read is not connecting with us on an emotional level.

People often mistake the phrase "write what you know" to mean specifically writing about themselves, but you do not have to write an autobiographical script in order to have a breakthrough piece of material. "Write what you know" means tapping into something you're familiar with and putting that on the page. Use those wounds in your own story and transfer them to your characters. At some point in your life, you experienced something worth writing about. The more honest you are, the more authentic your script will be, and the better it will represent you in the marketplace.

Netflix's *Unorthodox*[185] was partly based on Deborah Feldman escaping her life in the orthodox Jewish community. Although he was never an ad man in the '60s, Matt Wiener has said the idea for *Mad Men* came from his own personal struggle, wondering what do you do when you've achieved all of your goals? Whether you write directly about your life, or simply extract meaningful pieces from it to set yourself on the right course, bring the essence of who you are into your work.

As executives, we lean forward when scripts are relentlessly truthful.

---

[185] https://www.imdb.com/title/tt9815454/

YOUR VOICE

Using the term "voice" seems to stump many people. I'm not sure who came up with the phrase, but they didn't do anyone any favors. The simplest way to explain it is how you put words on a page.

When you look at all of your scripts, you will see a pattern in how you write. You might tend to write in a particular genre, format your scripts in a distinctive way, repeat phrasing or word choices, or return to certain character dynamics. You also might prefer to only write historical dramas or socially relevant content. All of these elements go into creating your voice.

Look at it this way: if you and ten other people were to be given the same writing prompt, each of you would come at the idea differently. Your specific way of approaching that prompt would reveal your voice.

When you think about Shonda Rhimes, your mind leaps to the dynamic, repetitive way her characters speak. Her shows are fast-paced, smart, and typically have a brilliant woman leading the charge. It's her signature style. It's the same with Ryan Murphy, Kenya Barris, and Lena Dunham. When you pick up a script with any of their names on it, you instantly know what you are getting, because the core of who they are comes out in their scripts. That is their voice.

Just read Misha Green's *The Mother*[186] and Tony Gilroy's *Bourne Identity,*[187] two action-thriller screenplays about spies on the run. Green's description comes in extremely

---

[186] https://www.imdb.com/title/tt6968614/
[187] https://www.imdb.com/title/tt0258463/

short sentences, never fully explaining the visuals of her locations or characters.

```
They strike like cougars.
At the same time.
He kicks her gun away.
She knocks his arm to the side.
```

Her script assumes we all know the shorthand of the genre, giving her the ability to dispense with the niceties of writing detailed description and instead get right down to business.

Gilroy demonstrates the lightning speed of Bourne's actions in a different way. Things are happening so fast that they've already taken place before we have had time to digest the movements.

```
COP #2 — writhing on the ground — gasping for
air — struggling with his holster — THE MAN —
his foot — down — like a vise — onto COP #2's
arm — shattering the bone — COP #2 starting to
scream, and then silenced because—
```

```
THE MAN — he's got the pistol — so fucking
fast — he's got it right up against COP #2's
forehead — right on the edge of pulling the
trigger — he is, he's gonna shoot him —
```

Same subject, different approach. Each one demonstrating the writers' voice. Mastering your voice gives us a reason to keep turning those pages.

THE HERO'S POINT OF VIEW

The hero of your show must have a perspective on the world unlike anyone else's. There should be clarity in the way they operate, so that we know that watching them will be a unique experience. In essence, they are our own personal tour guide through the world you have created for them. Witness Ted Lasso repeatedly confront the unrelenting cynicism of his team and the team's owner with undaunted optimism. His mantra "Believe" permeates every action he takes and every bit of advice he dispenses, which makes watching him butt up against the next person with a bad attitude so much fun. We look forward to seeing him turn a cranky adversary into a soft pile of mush. How he does it both captivates and enchants us.

We might not remember the plot of any particular episode of *Home Improvement,*[188] but we do remember Tim Allen grunting like a Neanderthal. You can drop Larry David's curmudgeonly character in *Curb Your Enthusiasm,* or *VEEP's*[189] hapless Selina Meyer, or the self-absorbed *Schitt's Creek*[190] family into any situation and know the comedy will come from how those characters interact with the world. It's Homer Simpson's dimwitted decisions that cause him to spin into ridiculous situations. Had he been more level-headed and reasonable, *The Simpsons* would be far less enjoyable.

You should be able to sum up your main character's philosophy about the world easily and succinctly. This will be your hero around whom you will create a team, and if you aren't sure who your lead is, your ensemble will fail to come together. *Mad Men's* Don Draper's smooth, misogynistic callousness walks us through the male-dominated world of advertising in the '60s. Eve Polastri's fan-girl exuberance in *Killing Eve*[191] pulls us into the MI-5 spy game

[188] https://www.imdb.com/title/tt0101120/
[189] https://www.imdb.com/title/tt1759761/
[190] https://www.imdb.com/title/tt3526078/
[191] https://www.imdb.com/title/tt7016936/

as she stalks Villanelle. Even *The Mandalorian,* [192] who exhibits little to no emotion, adheres to a draconian code of conduct.

Bones, Monk, and Sherlock may all use deductive reasoning to solve crimes, but we love them because their style and their philosophies are peculiar to them. Far beyond the situations these characters find themselves in, it's the manner in which they maneuver through the world that causes us to keep watching.

Now that you have a compelling main character, put that character in opposition to his world. Conflict equals story. *Silicon Valley* [193] explores the cut-throat world of tech. So, throwing an insecure and unsavvy developer into it is like tossing red meat to the lions. Where better to insert a mild-mannered, high school chemistry teacher than the drug trade? If Teresa in *Queen of the South* was already equipped to take over the cartel, there would be no drama in watching her rise. *The Walking Dead* could have been written through any other lens — an accountant, a barber, a thief — however a by-the-book sheriff thrust into a country overrun by lawlessness and the undead promises he'll be faced with moral decisions that will challenge him for seasons.

If your character isn't at odds with the world he/she is in, then you may have to adjust either the character or the concept. Series need conflict, and if everything is going along swimmingly for your lead, they have nothing to struggle against. Piper is the perfect character to enter into the women's penitentiary in *Orange is the New Black.*

---

[192] https://www.imdb.com/title/tt8111088/
[193] https://www.imdb.com/title/tt2575988/

She is a privileged fish out of water in a decidedly unprivileged prison system. She faces conflict at every turn, and watching her have to navigate her surroundings makes the show compelling. Had she already been a hardened criminal re-entering the system, the show wouldn't be nearly as interesting. It's precisely because she is new to this experience that we can enter into it with her and learn how to deal with the situation she now finds herself in.

Struggle is the stuff of which great stories are made. Force your hero into a terrible predicament. His flaws will be both his weakness and his strength. We will want to keep reading because how he maneuvers his way out should be intriguing, and we haven't seen it before in the specific way that you will tell this story.

There will be times when the idea you want to write simply refuses to come together. That's a great time to back up and reconsider exactly what you want to say. Start again, focusing on character and theme, and then build the world around that focal point. Once you know what you want to say about the world or man's condition in it, you can expand out from there. Sometimes, no matter how cool the idea may be, starting solely with concept can result in the idea feeling gimmicky. Don't be afraid to throw everything out and start over. Holding onto something that isn't working will only delay you getting to an even better idea down the line. You can always save what you have and come back to it later, but for the time being, begin fresh and ask yourself if it's really worth the agony to try to force the issue. If you can't answer the key questions about how it's working now, it really won't make sense when you try to explain it to someone else later.

THE HERO'S ENTRANCE

Take a look at the best pilots written in the last ten years and notice the commonalities of how they were put together. Great pilots give the main character a hero's entrance. Right away we are introduced to the world in which they operate and given insight into their particular point of view.

Scandal's Olivia Pope first burst onto the scene confidently negotiating the rescue of an infant in a take-no-prisoners style. In an early draft of the script, her entrance appears as:

```
EXT. WAREHOUSE DISTRICT — NIGHT

It's dirty and abandoned down here. An SUV
pulls up and OLIVIA (30s) steps out. Stylish
but weary, too smart for her own good. People
tend to underestimate her. That's a mistake.
STEPHEN (30s) is waiting for her. STEPHEN's
handsome and male and brilliant in a way
that makes you worried you'll do something
inappropriate like lick him. The minute she's
out of the car, they head for the warehouse.
All business, intense.
```

Moments later, Olivia boldly inserts herself between two gun-toting mobsters and fearlessly negotiates a truce, leaving with her package, a baby. Harrison has already recruited Quinn at a bar by telling her that he works for her idol, Olivia. Does she want to be a gladiator in a suit, he asks? Of course, she does!

With a setup like that, we instantly know that Olivia is formidable, one of the good guys, and the person anyone would want to follow into battle.

In *Ugly Betty*, unaware that she's a walking disaster, Betty unabashedly waits for an interview at a fashion magazine next to a gorgeous competitor.

```
Her. 24. Overweight. Bushy unibrow. Coke
bottle glasses. Hairspray caked bangs. If
beauty's defined by symmetry, Betty looks like
a bomb went off at Disney Hall. She nervously
clutches her briefcase as she sits inside...
```

Undaunted, Betty animatedly pitches herself to the HR rep who has just blown her off. Ultimately, it's Betty's determination that is both her flaw and her strength, as she's able to cut through pretense to speak her mind.

In the original version of *Murphy Brown,* Murphy didn't appear in the show right away, but the ensemble gave her a wind up before she even entered. Much like Miranda Priestly in *The Devil Wears Prada,* [194] we gleaned more from the way her co-workers behaved than we ever could have if she were to enter first. Before she even set foot in the office, we knew that she was just returning from a stint at Betty Ford, could not keep an assistant because they all kept quitting, and that she was a force to be reckoned with. NBC's *The Blacklist* [195] begins with Reddington boldly surrendering at FBI headquarters.

Treat your hero well. Give them a good entrance that tells us this is who we are following and why they are worth following into this world.

---

[194] https://www.imdb.com/title/tt0458352/

[195] https://www.imdb.com/title/tt2741602/

BUILDING AN ENSEMBLE

Game of Thrones[196] aside, development conventional wisdom says that anything beyond six characters in a core ensemble is confusing. After six and it's hard to keep everyone straight. Even more important than the number, each character must perform a very specific role within the ensemble. If they don't, they will get cycled out for a character who does.

Take a look at your pilot script. If you have more than six core characters, you might want to consider how each one interacts with your lead, and whether it's necessary to keep them in order to tell the stories you want to tell. Chances are, some of them are duplicating the voices of other characters and we will eventually ask you to kill one of them.

One way to develop your ensemble is to use personality tests like Myers-Briggs or DiSC assessments which break down the different personality types. My favorite book about character development is *People Patterns*[197] by Stephen Montgomery. In it, Montgomery lays out the four "temperaments," used as far back as the ancient Greeks, who believed that society was essentially made up of four personality types. Of course, like Myers-Briggs, there are variations of each type for a total of sixteen. At the end of his chapters, Montgomery also includes lists of movie characters that embody those traits. The assumption Montgomery makes is that people can be generally categorized into The Artisan, The Rational, The Guardian, and The Idealist.

---

[196] https://www.imdb.com/title/tt0944947/
[197] http://drstephenmontgomery.com/pp.html

I'll sum them up in extremely broad terms here, but there are many more layers and variations to explore, once you understand all of the different facets that go into comprising these types.

The Artisan tends to make rash decisions and believes that the end justifies the means. They'll get the result they want by any means necessary. These are fun characters to write because they are hard chargers, acting first, and thinking later, knowing that they'll be forgiven when all is said and done. Olivia Pope and Tony Soprano would most certainly be Artisans.

The Guardian is the protector and the rule follower who keeps everyone in line. Usually, the one who will remind the team that whatever they're about to do is against protocol. Rick Grimes would be the Guardian in *The Walking Dead.*

The Idealist is the people person of the group, genuine, earthy, perhaps even artistic. They are the dreamers and those who express love and hope. Think Phoebe Buffay from *Friends.*

The Rational believes in facts and figures, and can oftentimes be seen in a procedural as the techie reviewing the evidence and working the computer. Logical and analytical, they will provide the details and proof needed to accomplish the task at hand. Temperance Brennan in *Bones* is an excellent example of a Rational.

Your show may not have all four temperaments represented. In a comedy, the core group may only be three characters. However, when building your series, you want to make sure that every character serves a function, otherwise they will quickly find their way to the cutting room floor to allow time for the ones who do. When a supporting character tackles problems in the same way as the lead character, there's no need for them to exist. Do those characters give an opposing point of view that will be interesting when butting up against our lead character's unique stance?

Take a look at any procedural series, and you can easily see which character is which. The main character usually serves the role of the Artisan, with their Guardian partner urging them to stick to procedure. Tech support running the DNA samples fills the role of The Rational with the Idealist providing comic relief. There are always variations to each of these characters, and shows that find ways to turn the model on its head continue to freshen up the form. The main takeaway is that each member of your ensemble needs to provide a counterpoint to your central character. If they don't, it's time to consider losing them.

THE IMPORTANCE OF STAKES

Stakes appear in pilot scripts in two ways — in the personal stakes for your hero and in the story stakes of each episode.

Personal stakes are the emotional ties that answer the question who is your hero doing all of this for? David Chase brilliantly showed Tony Soprano in therapy and with his family before he ever showed us Tony beating a man half to death. His concern over his uncle using his friend's restaurant for a hit and placating his unreasonable mother indicate that, despite being a ruthless mobster, Tony still had feelings and was justified in his frustration.

Giving your hero someone to care for or who cares for them helps us buy into their journey. A child or an aging parent boosts the hero's resolve to accomplish whatever goal is in front of them. Whether family member, love interest, friend, or co-worker, whoever fills this need should be someone who will be a regular presence to keep the stakes high.

Story stakes invest us in the episode. Most pilots revolve around a life event — a birthday, wedding, anniversary, promotion, firing, reunion, death, or birth. Why? Because the character is emotionally invested in the outcome, which means we are invested. When stakes are low, we simply don't care as much. Look at the pilots of some of the most successful series. In *Friends*, Rachel flees her own wedding, showing up at Monica's hangout in her bridal gown. In *Cheers*, Diane is about to elope with Sumner when she meets Sam at the bar for the first time.

The most common pilot story is one centered around a birthday, universally recognized as the one day of the year for which everyone has expectations. We anticipate significant birthdays with joy or dread. We worry when we forget the birthdays of people we love. We desperately search for the right gifts, and when no one remembers ours, it hurts. Everyone is on the same page with why the day is important, so it shortcuts a need to bake in why the main character would care so much about it.

The *Black-ish*[198] pilot has both a promotion and a birthday, upping the ante considerably. The pilots of *The Sopranos, Breaking Bad,* and *Girlfriends* center on birthdays as well. Types of high stakes life events to consider are:

Birthday
Anniversary
Wedding
Promotion
New Job
Move
Death
Funeral
Birth
Losing a job

Try working with one of these areas to see if it sparks something for your lead character. These are simply jumping-off points to get started. Your script doesn't have to use any of those events. The important thing is to get us into the story and to care about what is happening as quickly as possible.

Procedurals have stakes already built into them. Medical, legal, and police shows are naturally about life and death situations. Will the doctor save the patient? Will the lawyer save the client? Will the detective save the next victim? These events immediately have us on the edge of our seats. But we still need to know why your main character cares so much about making the save. Beyond the person they are rescuing, what's in it for them?

---

[198] https://www.imdb.com/title/tt3487356/

USE YOUR VERBS

When you're confident on the page, we take notice. Knowing that we're in capable hands gives us a sense of security as we read your script. One of the markers of strong storytelling is the effective use of description. Do yourself a favor and download a copy of the *Breaking Bad* pilot, which pretty much everyone in Hollywood agrees is one of the best examples of sensational writing. Vince Gilligan's script immediately gives us a clear idea of the main character, the stakes, tone, urgency, and even color scheme of the series. But Gilligan does something else — he uses incredibly energetic verbs. Read the first five pages, and then go back and circle each of them. Here are just a few that I pulled onto a list.

Graze
Rolling
Buzz
Zoom
Speeding
Roaring
Stumbles
Leaps
Yanks
Clutched
Grabs
Tucks
Bottoms out
Plow
Kicks open

Gilligan could have used the word "opens" instead of "yanks," "held" instead of "clutched," or "exits" instead of "stumbles," but he didn't. Passive verbs and overusing the word "is" slows down a read, taking all of the specificity and attitude out of the description. Gilligan chose the most dynamic verbs that conveyed the frantic actions of a desperate man.

LIMIT YOUR SETTINGS

While it should not be the driving force behind your creative process, being conscious of your pilot's settings can be helpful. For sure, your studio is thinking about this as the script edges closer to getting a pick-up. They will want to know that they can produce your show for whatever amount of money they've allotted for your budget.

Unlike a feature film which can theoretically travel all over the world, television shows typically live in a finite number of locations and settings. If it's a workplace show, the office will be the primary set. If it's a family show, the central home will be where most of the action plays out. Beyond the main location, you may have a handful of other regular places that you will likely revisit within the seven to ten days of production for each episode. Unless you're writing a roadshow, select places you can have your characters come back to again and again during the course of the series.

OPEN WITH A BANG

Lost[199] opens in the seconds after a plane crash, with scared, injured, and dying passengers littering the beach as Jack

---

[199] https://www.imdb.com/title/tt0411008/

races to get them out of harm's way. Within moments of the start of *Desperate Housewives*, [200] Mary Alice Young shoots herself in the head. Eleanor Shellstrop learns she is dead thirty-three seconds into the pilot of *The Good Place*. [201] Most cop shows begin with a body dump, and right from jump, medical shows introduce an emergency.

Hook us early with a riveting teaser and you will have us in your grip. Subvert our expectations. Show us that you are one step ahead of us and are going to deliver something new. There's a picture I like to use as an example of switching things up. A housewife stands in her kitchen. She's wearing an apron, surrounded by mixing bowls and a rolling pin dusted with flour, having just baked a pie that is now in the oven behind her. The look on her face is matter-of-fact as she's finishing up her new task . . . polishing her AR-15.

I'm intrigued by the image. I want to know who this woman is and what she's preparing for. And I want to know right now. While outwardly she adheres to outdated conventions of a woman's role in the household, she quite clearly runs much deeper on the inside, ready to take care of business, whatever that turns out to be. Is her husband in on her plan or is he the target of her impending wrath? What if she's married to a woman or single and all of this is just a cover? What is the world like outside of her kitchen door? Are we in the past, present, or future? When you set up something we think we're going to know the answer to, and then change it up almost as quickly, we can't help but go on the ride with you.

---

[200] https://www.imdb.com/title/tt0410975/
[201] https://www.imdb.com/title/tt4955642/

Download the pilot for *Homeland.* The opening scene begins with two soldiers erecting a gallows inside a prison courtyard. We cut to Carrie weaving through traffic in a race against time to get intel from a source she's not even sure is reliable. She's promised to help him protect his family, but she's run out of time. He whispers something into her ear just as she's whisked away by the guards and he's carted off to his death.

It's a thrilling opening. We have to keep reading to learn who, why, and how the rest of this plays out.

This isn't to say that your first few pages have to deliver a high energy shock-fest, but we need to be intrigued enough to keep reading your script. Page 1 of the *This is Us*[202] pilot sets us up for the idea that there may be a connection between those who share the same birthdate. By page 2, we meet a naked Jack and his pregnant wife Rebecca, who goes into labor by page 4. The opening couldn't be more different from *Homeland,* the tone sweeter and quieter, but no less captivating. Find a way to pull us in and you've got a good chance of getting us on your side.

---

[202] https://www.imdb.com/title/tt5555260/

CHAPTER 8

NOTES

*I*f just reading the word "notes" on this page sends you into a tailspin, this chapter is most certainly for you. No writer likes getting notes, and execs don't like giving them, but they're a necessary part of the process which, in success, gets you closer to your goal: getting your script made. Understanding the executive mindset about notes, and learning how to take them well, can help ease the pain of this important step.

Television development is all about collaboration. Everyone will have notes about how to make your idea better. Those notes usually come with good intentions and are based on the note giver's likes and dislikes, the things they've been taught, and their past experiences with other projects. From an executive's point of view, they are here to help, not hurt your project. No exec goes into a notes meeting with the intent to destroy what you've created. They're invested in what you've written, and, even if it doesn't feel like it, they truly want you to succeed.

Writers often resist notes they think will unravel their entire idea so when someone "bumps" on a particular aspect of the story, they fight hard to retain what they've already built rather than consider rebuilding it from scratch. The reaction is completely understandable, particularly with intricate plots that are carefully assembled. If one piece is removed or one thread pulled, the entire idea falls apart. However, if your reader finds themselves losing interest in your script, or unable to understand what's going on, you need to know that.

TAKING NOTES WELL

If you can learn to hear a note without getting defensive, you'll be way ahead of the game. Try to hear past how the note is delivered and dig into why they are giving you the note in the first place. Something isn't clear or isn't resonating in your script. These are fixable issues. How you address the problem is up to you. And no matter what note you get, even if you play around with it and hate what you've come up with, you can always go back to your earlier draft.

Whoever is giving you notes should start with what they love about your writing. You need to hear what you did well, what characters they loved, and that your work landed, otherwise, you won't hear anything else they say. Putting yourself out there for criticism is hard to do and when the work you do isn't acknowledged up front, you will probably internalize it as a negative. Do your best to keep in mind that notes are not personal attacks on who you are, but rather vehicles to make your work better.

Let's assume, for a moment, that your dialogue is transcendent. You are the next Aaron Sorkin! We'll set that aside for now and focus on the mechanics of the story. There are many reasons why people give notes, but here are couple of the biggies. Either your script hasn't given them enough information along the way to get your characters from point A to point B, you haven't earned the moments that you need to get your reader emotionally invested, or you've given us too much information that doesn't need to be there. We want to go along for the ride with you. Take us with you.

One particularly helpful notes technique my Sundance mentor used with me involved "going up the mountain." What if, she asked, we looked at the concept in an entirely different way and took the time to play it out. So, rather than fighting to keep a stranglehold on what I had, I "went up the mountain" with her, imagining a different scenario to see if it worked. In my own script, going up the mountain confirmed for me something I hadn't wanted to admit – my A and B stories should be flipped. The romantic B story was actually the emotional heart of the script. It contained an even deeper thematic message than my work-related A story. By turning my B story into my A story, my script became less analytical and much more emotionally satisfying.

There are times, however, that going up the mountain reveals something you've suspected, but have been afraid to acknowledge — that your script requires more work than you want to do. When that happens, you will have to make a choice. Are you going to dig in your heels and stick to what you have? Or are you going to rethink everything and maybe stumble upon something even better?

I call my own notes giving process "sitting on the floor and pulling it apart." I'll admit, it's not the most elegant term, but it is exactly what it says. Sitting on the floor. I started using the phrase after Marc Cherry came into my office to pitch me the opening to *Desperate Housewives*. My producing partner and I had both known Marc for years and had been out pitching a half-hour comedy with him about his mother which we were unable to sell. This time, though, he had a more dramatic take. Marc came in, sat on my office floor, and proceeded to pitch me the most amazing opening to a show I'd ever heard. He detailed Mary Alice Young's perfectly organized kitchen and her final, regimented moments on earth before she did the unexpected and shot herself.

Unfortunately, Paramount didn't want to buy it, so my partner and I lost out on working with Marc on one of the most iconic series ever created. For me, though, there was something refreshing about seeing things from a totally new vantage point. Literally sitting on the floor brings me a new perspective when I need it most. It can reboot the creative process when things seem to reach a stumbling block.

A few years ago, I worked on a particularly challenging project and asked the writer to come sit on the floor with me to pull it apart. There was something about looking at the pages of his script as if we were children playing Legos, that helped us both see things differently. When I received the next draft, I was astounded. I sent it to two literary agents and within a week, he was signed by one of the top agencies in town. Six days later, he had three offers to staff.

That won't be everyone's story, but it is one example of how being open to the notes process can yield a much-needed breakthrough.

Whether you agree with a note or not, you need to be able to openly listen to, decode, and respond to notes in order to keep you moving in the right direction. The last thing any executive wants to do is to give notes to a bad note taker. We dread every second of it. There are a handful of very prominent writers in town who are notoriously challenging to give notes to. Their past experiences with executives have left them defensive and argumentative, even when the notes they are getting are valid and could make their scripts better. These writers fall into the "life's too short" category. They may be wildly successful, but no exec wants to have the misfortune of being chewed out for giving a note that most likely came from someone much higher up the food chain.

When a show is in production, the note giving task falls to the Current executive, one of the most underrated positions in the business. The Current exec is the one keeping the show on track. They watch every cut, read every script, and deliver every single note. It's a tremendous amount of work and doesn't always come with the types of kudos enjoyed by those in development.

PUSHING BACK

Sometimes bad notes happen. I find that execs a little on the greener side, or ones who have never experienced how tough it is to sell a project, don't always understand what it takes for a writer to be vulnerable on a page. They might phrase things awkwardly or not be able to get to the point, beating around the bush when a simple straightforward criticism would be so much easier.

I once worked with an executive who had a hard time completing a sentence. Every time he started to say something, he'd trail off as if the next part of what he was going to say was obvious, so why say it? The problem was, nothing he said was obvious, and so we were often left with only half a thought and had to hope we were all assuming we were on the same page. We never were.

I've heard horror stories from writers detailing notes calls with fifteen executives, each one feeling the need to weigh in. How can that possibly be productive? On the one hand, it means that the team is invested in that script and everyone wants to put their fingerprints on it; however, as far as I'm concerned, it means the team leader has not wrangled the process effectively on their end. One primary note giver with maybe a few other voices to add context or emphasis is all you really need. Anything more than that is overkill.

Here's a secret: you do not have to take every note that's ever given to you. Crazy concept, right? It's true. All notes are not good notes. You do, however, have to listen to all notes with an open mind. Something in your work is making your reader ask you to clarify something. The key is hearing the note. Take the spirit of the note more than the actual note itself. You might not have to unravel everything if what they are really bumping on can be accomplished in another way. Your exec may even say, "Here's the bad version," fully acknowledging that they don't have a fix for you, but are pinpointing a problem, even if their solution is a terrible example that you would never use.

Use the phrases "I'll take a look at that" and "I tried it and it didn't work." Executives know that when you say these two things, they're politely being blown off, but it doesn't matter. This is a way for everyone to save face, even when you don't want to take a note. It's a win-win for everyone. Executives need to know that you have heard their thoughts and that you have tried to implement them, even if you are dead set against it. And you, as the writer, will want to seem as collaborative as you can for the sake of your relationship. "I'll take a look at that," simply means that you will consider the note. That's it.

"I tried it and it didn't work," is what you say when you've delivered your next draft and the change the exec asked for isn't in it. Just tell them that you tried to make their note work, but for some reason it just didn't fit in the script. We all know that you may or may not have tried, but it makes us feel good that you heard the thought and considered it, even if in the end, you rejected it.

Receiving a note you hate can be easier said than done. My advice? Use that phrase "I'll take a look at that," and pay attention to what we call "the note under the note."

THE NOTE UNDER THE NOTE

Execs don't want to confuse you on purpose, and yet sometimes cryptic phrases leap out of our mouths and we forget to explain to you exactly what we mean. We're just so used to speaking amongst ourselves, that we don't stop to think that maybe it doesn't make sense to anyone else. When we say something that just begs to be decoded, it's okay for you to ask us to elaborate. We're perfectly happy to give you the low down.

Here are a few standard notes that executives give which tend to confuse writers and fall into the category of "executive-speak."

CAN YOU MAKE YOUR CHARACTER MORE LIKEABLE?

This is the note you will get when your exec isn't on board with your main character. There are many arguments for and against the likable hero, but one thing is for certain, it's very hard to remain engaged in a series if you don't at least understand where the main character is coming from. We're introduced to Ray Donavan[203] when he calmly instructs a panicked client on how to deal with the dead girl in his bed. "You think you're the first person I've dealt with woke up in bed with a dead body?" Ray says. But even as we see Ray's questionable morals at play, we also discover he is hyper-protective of his own family.

In *Curb Your Enthusiasm*, Larry David could not be more disagreeable, and yet, he's endlessly entertaining, saying exactly what we would be thinking if put in the same situation.

In the opening of *House of Cards*[204] Frank Underwood puts a dog out of its misery. It is a truly despicable act and yet we are fascinated by his thinking and intrigued by his methods. In the following few minutes, he lovingly clasps a necklace around his wife's neck, and strolls through a

[203] https://www.imdb.com/title/tt2249007/
[204] https://www.imdb.com/title/tt1856010/

gala introducing himself as our savvy chaperone into the unsavory world of Washington politics. We're hooked.

We show up to a television series to see characters we love do something in a very specific, distinctive way. It doesn't matter where they do it, or even what they are doing, so long as how they do it surprises and delights us. As long as your hero's point of view is clearly drawn and we empathize with their situation, you shouldn't have to worry about whether they are likable or not. Dexter was a serial killer, and yet, because we understood his logic, we eagerly watched him dispatch the bad guys who skirted the system. His justice was our justice.

This gets us back to those personal stakes. Show your hero — no matter how loathsome — loving, loving someone, or being loved, and you are on your way to diffusing this note.

YOU'RE PUTTING A HAT ON A HAT

Also known as "putting spin on spin." This note is aimed at getting you to focus on only what is necessary. By adding too much to an idea, the script becomes convoluted. If your hero is both a doctor and a lawyer who also races cars underwater, you may have tried to do too much. Pull it back so that we have a clear idea of what you are trying to convey. Sometimes, much less is more.

YOUR CHARACTER NEEDS A WIN EARLY ON

When characters are seen as being good at something, we are more apt to get behind them. The moment we first see Jake in *Brooklyn Nine-Nine,* [205] even though he is cracking

---

[205] https://www.imdb.com/title/tt2467372/

jokes and seems to take absolutely nothing seriously, he also demonstrates that he's a fantastic detective by solving a case.

The Mandalorian proves he's a skilled fighter and merciless bounty hunter before we've even hit the pilot's four-minute mark.

In *Damages,* [206] high-stakes litigator Patty Hewes plays hardball with her competition, refusing to compromise until he agrees to her settlement price. She does it with humor and compassion, going so far as to evoke the memory of the young client she is fighting for. A few scenes later, Patty's colleague, Tom, describes Patty as living and dying by instinct, never tolerating phoniness. We now know that not only is Patty the best at what she does, her secret weapon is her ability to read her competition.

DO WE REALLY NEED . . . ?

If you're getting the "do we really need" note, your exec is asking for trims. Your script might be dragging or the character they want to ax isn't serving the intended function and needs to be reworked. Either way, at some point, they found themselves having to white knuckle it through your script to get to the good part. If the issue is pace, ask yourself if the scene is only there to deliver exposition. If it is, look for a way to slide that info in somewhere else. Or see if you can twist the scene so that what happens in it is less expected. If the problem is with a character, look to see if that attitude is a duplicate of another character's POV. Don't be afraid to kill a character if it isn't working. It will give you time to put toward the ones that are.

---

[206] https://www.imdb.com/title/tt0914387/

CAN YOU FIND A BETTER BLOW TO THIS SCENE?

We're looking for a funnier joke at the end of your scene. If the moment isn't landing, it might be due to the phrasing, you may have drifted off story, not surprised us enough by the reversal, or you've given the best line to someone other than your lead. Try saying the words out loud to see if they work. If it doesn't make you laugh, beat what you have with a better out.

CAN WE FIND A STRONGER ACT BREAK?

You'll get this note more in broadcast or basic cable, which still has act breaks, but even if you're writing for premium cable or the streamers, the act structure still holds. As your script progresses, there should be a series of escalations and reversals that keep your audience off-balance. Leaving a scene on a cliff-hanger is a good way to keep us engaged.

4 WAYS OF PASSING, WHEN WE DON'T WANT TO SAY WE'RE PASSING

- **WE DON'T LOVE IT** — This is a gentle way of saying we didn't like whatever you did. Saying "we don't like it" seems much meaner than "we don't love it," which can mean we like aspects of it, but overall, it wasn't resonating with us enough to push it forward.

- **WE JUST DIDN'T GET IT** — Maybe the writing was confusing, or you built an overly complicated world. This could also mean that what you think is funny isn't funny to us.

- **IT'S NOT WHAT WE'RE LOOKING FOR RIGHT NOW** — The script is not fitting into any of the genres we are interested in or filling any scheduling needs.

- **WE HAVE SOMETHING JUST LIKE IT IN DEVEL-OPMENT** — Networks don't like to double develop ideas, making it unlikely that we will want to buy the same idea twice. Even when you think your version is different, if there is enough overlap between them, we won't bite. On the other hand, if David E. Kelley brings in an idea that's close to something we've already bought from a lesser-known writer, we'll most certainly back up the Brink's truck.

DON'T TAKE IT PERSONALLY

You send your script to an exec and don't hear back for months. What's up with that? You're putting yourself out there. Common decency insists that you should hear something, right? Wrong. Getting feedback on your material is hard, but what's even harder is not getting any feedback at all. Do not take the deafening, soul-crushing, horrible silence personally. Not hearing back is not always about you. Most of the time it's about us. Take a breath. Here's what is most likely happening.

1) **We simply haven't read it yet.** We get a gargantuan number of scripts sent to us every week, and unless we have extra time or your title is wildly intriguing, your script may get pushed to the bottom of the stack as more important material is sent to our inboxes. We might also lose the script in that growing inbox. Or we may have read the first few pages and then forgot to finish. We need a strong enough reason to go back and read your work. You sending a gentle reminder email, having your rep or some advocate we trust give us a call, or you gaining momentum elsewhere will light a fire under us to get it done.

2) **We liked it and we've already passed it on to someone else.** Everyone in the business is running at full tilt all of the time and the last thing they have on their minds is whether they remembered to email you back to tell you how amazing you are when you thought they should. Things are incredibly important to you because, in your line of sight, your script is everything. But for an executive, we're thinking about our own growing list of priorities. If we don't remember to reach out, it doesn't mean that nothing is happening. If your script is great, we're sharing it with our colleagues and showrunners. We don't always call you to tell you what we're doing, but there's a chance that the backchannel is already at work.

3) **We didn't connect with your material.** Sometimes it happens. Not every script is for every exec, and having to pass is hard, which is why we do our best to dodge the inevitable. You might never know that we didn't love the script because that silence means we've already moved onto other things.

4) **Bad timing.** We like your script, but it's just not for us right now. Today our mandate is to find YA comedies for an 18–34-year-old audience, and you write dark, brooding dramas. Maybe it's just not a fit this moment, but six months from now when we're staffing a show about a serial killer, we'll want to reach out to you.

Good or bad, when receiving notes, here's one final piece of advice that helps every time. Get them in writing. When you ask for notes on a page, it forces the executives to be judicious with their thoughts. Fifteen people on a notes call is absolute insanity, but when those fifteen people are forced to look at all of those notes on one document, some things will drop off just because the sheer tonnage of bullet points on that page will look ridiculous. Only the most important notes will remain. You will also be able to respond to them on paper when you are done. Type in non-threatening blue font how you either addressed the thought or "tried it and it didn't work."

Recording the notes works well, too, although the notes givers will still feel free to ramble on ad nauseam and you won't be able to reply as efficiently. What it does is gives you a chance to listen dispassionately, knowing you can always go back and listen again and again, to make sure you've heard the note under the note. Give yourself a day or two to to digest the notes then return to your script, having had a little distance.

Ultimately, it boils down to this: executives want to know that they have been heard. They want to feel included, just as you wanted to feel included in their process by selling your script. How do you do that? Make a small, but noticeable change on page one. Psychologically, it tells the executive that you are willing to make changes to your work. Things are not set in stone. It can be cosmetic. Add a joke they haven't heard before. Switch up the description. Give them some indication that you are listening and yes, your script did benefit from hearing them. Even if you don't wind up doing every note they've asked you for, you remain flexible and someone they want to work with. Be the writer they want to ask back.

Now, if none of that works for you and you refuse to take any note because you don't want to play in the industry sandbox, well, you're on your own.

CHAPTER 9

CONGRATS! YOU'VE SOLD YOUR SCRIPT!

*A*pplause and kudos! You've made it through the initial gauntlet and have been commissioned to write your script. Congratulations! This is a huge moment, so take it in. However, this is where the stakes get higher, and it's more important than ever to get it right. The first order of business is making your deal.

Most deals for emerging writers are if/come. Once you have a credit behind you, they may give you money to develop your show before pitching to the network or, when you become a seasoned writer, you might be offered a first look or an overall deal. Here are a few terms you may need to know about deals:

IF/COME — All of the work you do on this project is on spec. You only get paid if you sell the project to a network. Sometimes described as "if you sell it, then comes the money."

BLIND SCRIPT DEAL — A blind script means the studio or network has faith that you will deliver an idea to them, even if you don't have an idea yet. All they know right now is that they want to work with you. Together you'll figure out what the show is.

FIRST-LOOK DEAL — A first-look gives the studio or network the first right of refusal to any projects from that writer. If the project is passed on, then the writer can take that project elsewhere to sell it.

HOUSEKEEPING DEAL — When a studio gives you a housekeeping deal as part of your first-look, it also it guarantees to cover your office expenses. This might include office space, assistant, and costs of maintaining that office (computer, printer, etc.), as well as reimbursement for meals. Whenever you sell a project, you are given a cash bonus.

OVERALL DEAL — More seasoned writers negotiate larger deals that start in the millions. It takes you completely off the market, only working with one studio or network. These are typically multi-year deals that tie you up for some time. In return, you are expected to develop ideas solely for that one studio or net, and will probably be put to work on a show for that company. The advantage of getting locked up and paid such a good amount of money is that you have the ability to build a company and hire a team to help develop more content. Given the high rate of failure in the business, having more irons in the fire gives this deal an advantage.

POD DEAL — This is the same as an overall, but the term means Producer Overall Deal. These can be made directly with a writer or producer with a production company. The studio is making a deal with the entity itself.

For a general idea of how much these kinds of deals would make, check out the WGA schedule of minimums on their website.

WRITING YOUR FORMAT OR BIBLE

While you may or may not wind up sharing any of this with your network, you will want to have a roadmap of your series. This is called your format or bible. The difference between the two is basically semantics, although guild rules prohibit a buyer from commissioning extensive work without payment, so "format" often becomes the preferred terminology. Formats are typically shorter than bibles, but they are both documents that ensure whoever is working on your show is on the same page as you about what you are producing.

Included in the format is the overview of your idea, the theme, setting, tone, and characters with complete backstories. You should also add story ideas, season arcs, and your series arc to give a sense of where the show is going over time. Does your idea employ a particular style? Explain that as well. You may want to use flashbacks, flash-forwards, or special effects, whatever important information you need to give, making it crystal clear that's what you intend to do. If the world you are creating is complex, world-building, futuristic, or requires more detail and depth than a simple conversation can relay, the format will make clear to everyone exactly what you sold and how you plan to execute it.

How you format your bible and how long it becomes is up to you. Bibles can be eight pages, thirty pages, or like David Simon's bible for *The Wire*, a detailed seventy-eight pages. Ultimately, you may decide not to do one at all. Your idea might be fully formed in your head and you can write a script perfectly fine without one.

WAITING FOR YOUR PICK-UP

Once your final draft is into the network, all that's left to do is wait. You are now in contention with everyone else who has also been in development for a pilot pick up. At this point, your studio may be trying to attach talent or a director to your script to make the package more enticing. If there is ever a time for you to lean on your relationships with big names that might make a difference, it's now, but only if they've been approved by the network. The last thing you want to do is to attach to your show someone they aren't wild about.

This is an excruciating time. You might get hints that you are a frontrunner in the pilot sweepstakes, or hear the unbearable phrase "you're in the mix" which means just that, you're still in contention, but not at the top of the list. They'll wait until all of their other scripts come in before making a firm decision.

During this time, you'll start to make plans, even if they're only in your head. You'll imagine who will direct, what actors you'll cast, where you'll shoot your pilot, and what crew you'll hire.

And when you finally get that call you've been waiting for, the dream becomes a reality. "Congrats! You're picked up to pilot!"

CHAPTER 10

FINAL THOUGHTS

*I*f you take away only one piece of information from this book, it's that development executives are just the other side of the creative process. We love content, story, character, and working in the industry just like you. If you're passionate enough about storytelling and committed enough to endure the inevitable setbacks, you can make a living in this business. And if someone like me, whose parents worked in dentistry, could worm her way in and stick it out for over thirty years, you can too. Whether you wind up writing, directing, on a crew, or in an executive chair, there are a multitude of resources available to assist you at every point in your career. Take advantage of as many of them as you can, build your network, and continue to perfect your craft.

The most important thing is that you stick with it and keep yourself open to what your career could look like. This business changes quickly, and what might be "the thing" today might be old news tomorrow. So long as you're flexible and keep moving forward, you will do just fine.

Keep your eye on what you are doing. As soon as you get even a little forward movement, we will come around.

If you get a meeting elsewhere, let us know. Someone else has validated you, which is meaningful all around. It might seem like it's hedging our bets, because it is, but we all do it when we pick a new series to watch. We choose what to spend time on, weighing factors such as who wrote and stars in it, to whether we like the concept and how long it will take us to consume it. If other people whose taste you value say it's good, you're much more likely to check it out. We only have so much time in the day, so why not be selective on how to use it?

The last thing I'll offer you is this: You can fix everything in post. I'm the perfect example of how, even though you might travel down one path, you can always veer onto another. It took me thirty-some years to get back onto the writing side of the business, but it happened. Along the way, I learned valuable lessons about the industry that I'm only able to share with you because I made that detour. In all that time, I never stopped working on my craft, taking writing and improv classes, reading scripts, going to movies, watching web series, and bingeing shows.

I still practice pitching with people I trust to give me good feedback, and share my work with other writers who deliver notes that challenge me to do better. I force myself to approach new faces at the hors d'oeuvres table, and I create grids to remind myself to follow up just enough so that I still pass the crazy test.

Writing is a life-long relationship with words and ideas. It requires passion and commitment, hope, and loads of creativity. But where else can we let our imagination roam wild, conjure up characters, blow up the world or save it, rewrite history or create a new future? In what other business can being honest and vulnerable cause a ripple effect through someone else's life?

When the words you write become images on screen, you change how others experience life. A few years ago, I moderated a panel about the next generation of executives. One of my last questions to the guest speakers was to describe what they loved about the creative process. One of the up-and-coming creative execs said that she gravitated toward development because her immigrant mother barely spoke English. Television, the exec said, was her way of translating the world for her. After that answer, I was a puddle. What a beautiful way to speak about what we do. We translate the world for each other.

Best of luck to you in your endeavors. As I said at the start of this, don't waste time worrying about what might or might not happen, or whether you're good enough to go the distance right this second. Spend it being as wildly creative as you can. Do the work, study the craft, be nice to people, listen to notes even if you don't wind up taking them, and enjoy telling stories. This is a journey. It might take a minute. But in in order for you to bring out your unique and fearless voice, you need to stay the course.

After all, the next *Game of Thrones* isn't going to write itself.

ABOUT THE AUTHOR

KELLY EDWARDS has worked for every major studio in Hollywood. After a long career as a film and television executive, she decided to blow up her life and become a writer. It was the best move she ever made.

Edwards holds a B.A. in Theater from Vassar and a MFA in Writing for Film and Television from Emerson College. She has been a Sundance Episodic Lab fellow and raised three amazingly brilliant daughters. She currently writes for the Fox drama *Our Kind Of People* and splits her time between Los Angeles and Missoula, Montana where she has recently taken up ice-fishing.

http://www.kellyedwards.co/
info@kellyedwards.co

THE WRITER'S JOURNEY
MYTHIC STRUCTURE FOR WRITERS

25TH ANNIVERSARY EDITION

CHRISTOPHER VOGLER

Originally an influential memo Vogler wrote for Walt Disney Animation executives regarding *The Lion King*, The Writer's Journey details a twelve-stage, myth-inspired method that has galvanized Hollywood's treatment of cinematic storytelling. A format that once seldom deviated beyond a traditional three-act blueprint, Vogler's comprehensive theory of story structure and character development has met with universal acclaim, and is detailed herein using examples from myths, fairy tales, and classic movies. This book has changed the face of screenwriting worldwide over the last 25 years, and continues to do so.

"This book is like having the smartest person in the story meeting come home with you and whisper what to do in your ear as you write a screenplay. Insight for insight, step for step, Chris Vogler takes us through the process of connecting theme to story and making a script come alive."
—Lynda Obst, producer, How to Lose a Guy in 10 Days, Sleepless in Seattle, One Fine Day, Contact; Author, Hello, He Lied

"The Writer's Journey is an insightful and even inspirational guide to the craft of storytelling. An approach to structure that is fresh and contemporary, while respecting our roots in mythology."
—Charles Russell, writer, director, producer, Dreamscape, The Mask, Eraser

"The Writer's Journey should be on anyone's bookshelf who cares about the art of storytelling at the movies. Not just some theoretical tome filled with development clichés of the day, this book offers sound and practical advice on how to construct a story that works."
—David Friendly, producer, Little Miss Sunshine, Daylight, Courage Under Fire, Out to Sea, My Girl

CHRISTOPHER VOGLER made documentary films as an Air Force officer before studying film production at the University of Southern California, where he encountered the ideas of mythologist Joseph Campbell and observed how they influenced the story design of 1977's *Star Wars*. He worked as a story consultant in the development departments of 20th Century Fox, Walt Disney Pictures and Animation, and Paramount Pictures, and wrote an influential memo on Campbell's Hero's Journey concept that led to his involvement in Disney's *Aladdin, The Lion King*, and *Hercules*. After the publication of *The Writer's Journey*, he developed stories for many productions, including Disney's remake of *101 Dalmatians*, Fox's *Fight Club, Courage Under Fire, Volcano*, and *The Thin Red Line*.

$29.95 · 400 PAGES · ISBN: 9781615933150

MICHAEL WIESE PRODUCTIONS

IN A DARK TIME, a light bringer came along, leading the curious and the frustrated to clarity and empowerment. It took the well-guarded secrets out of the hands of the few and made them available to all. It spread a spirit of openness and creative freedom, and built a storehouse of knowledge dedicated to the betterment of the arts.

The essence of Michael Wiese Productions (MWP) is empowering people who have the burning desire to express themselves creatively. We help them realize their dreams by putting the tools in their hands. We demystify the sometimes secretive worlds of screenwriting, directing, acting, producing, film financing, and other media crafts.

By doing so, we hope to bring forth a realization of 'conscious media,' which we define as being positively charged, emphasizing hope, and affirming positive values like trust, cooperation, self-empowerment, freedom, and love. Grounded in the deep roots of myth, it aims to be healing both for those who make the art and those who encounter it. It hopes to be transformative for people, opening doors to new possibilities and pulling back veils to reveal hidden worlds.

MWP has built a storehouse of knowledge unequaled in the world, for no other publisher has so many titles on the media arts. Please visit www.mwp.com, where you will find many free resources and a 25% discount on our books. Sign up and become part of the wider creative community!

MICHAEL WIESE, Co-Publisher
GERALDINE OVERTON, Co-Publisher

ᒥᐤ

CPSIA information can be obtained
at www.ICGtesting.com
Printed in the USA
JSHW030900230921
18931JS00001B/1